Praise for *Spy*

"Lie detection isn't ingrained; it's learned. . . . By following their advice, which is based off years of interrogating terrorists and double agents, anyone can improve their odds at getting to the truth."

—*New York Post*

"Michael Floyd and two fellow former agents, with more than seventy-five years of interrogation experience between them, honed their methods on terrorists and criminals. But their advice works equally well on cheating spouses, lollygagging employees, or schoolkids feigning illness."   —*Star Tribune*

"This book is both entertaining and highly informative—and it's the real deal. It gives readers genuine practical tools and tactics to use in all walks of life. I highly recommend it."

—David J. Lieberman, Ph.D., *New York Times* bestselling author of *Never Be Lied to Again*

"For many years, Phil and his team have employed their skills to vet terrorist sources, catch spies, and protect the nation's secrets. With this book, they have done something perhaps even more remarkable: equip anyone to reliably detect deception. Consciously or not, we all judge others' sincerity and truthfulness to protect ourselves. Most of us do it badly. This book will teach you to do it well."

—Robert Grenier, chairman of ERG Partners, former director of the CIA Counterterrorism Center

"In this entertaining, instructive, and fascinating book, Phil, Michael, and Susan lay out an easy-to-follow process for detecting deception, with real-life stories that are the stuff of spy novels. I have used their model for years with phenomenal results."

—Marisa R. Randazzo, Ph.D., managing partner at
SIGMA Threat Management Associates,
former chief research psychologist, U.S. Secret Service

"When my detectives on the LAPD's Counterterrorism Bureau and Robbery-Homicide Division took the course, we had veteran investigators tell us, 'No one should ever be promoted to the rank of detective without taking this course,' and 'I now want to go back and re-interview every suspect I ever questioned.' What this team has developed is truly unique, and anyone can learn to use it."

—Bill Bratton, senior advisor at Kroll Associates,
former LAPD chief, former NYPD and
Boston Police Department commissioner

SPY THE LIE

FORMER CIA OFFICERS TEACH YOU HOW TO DETECT DECEPTION

Philip Houston, Michael Floyd,
& Susan Carnicero with Don Tennant

ST. MARTIN'S GRIFFIN ✦ NEW YORK

For those who have sacrificed in service to a noble cause

SPY THE LIE. Copyright © 2012 by Philip Houston, Michael Floyd, Susan Carnicero, and Don Tennant. All rights reserved. Printed in the United States of America. For information, address St. Martin's Press, 175 Fifth Avenue, New York, N.Y. 10010.

www.stmartins.com

Design by Steven Seighman

The Library of Congress has cataloged the hardcover edition as follows:

Spy the lie : former CIA officers show you how to detect deception /
Philip Houston . . . [et al.].
    p. cm
  ISBN 978-1-250-00585-4 (hardcover)
  ISBN 978-1-250-00975-3 (e-book)
 1. Lie detectors and detection.   I. Houston, Philip.
  HV8078.S66 2012
  155.2'32—dc23

                            2012009737

ISBN 978-1-250-02962-1 (trade paperback)

St. Martin's Griffin books may be purchased for educational, business, or promotional use. For information on bulk purchases, please contact Macmillan Corporate and Premium Sales Department at 1-800-221-7945 extension 5442 or write specialmarkets@macmillan.com.

CONTENTS

ACKNOWLEDGMENTS

This book is in large part the culmination of a body of work performed by a lot of people whose names aren't on the cover, made possible in even larger part by the loving support of our families. The encouragement and advice of the people in our lives who are closest to us, along with their unflinching willingness to share the burdens that necessarily accompany any meaningful endeavor, lie at the heart of everything that went in to an effort that has spanned several years.

Throughout this process we have been surrounded by individuals who have demonstrated not only a gracious generosity with their time and expertise, but a genuine desire to help make this book a worthy voice of subject matter that can truly change people's lives for the better. We are especially grateful for the able guidance of Peter Romary, an internationally recognized legal expert and a valued friend and colleague who serves as a partner in QVerity, the company we founded to advance and share the concepts we've presented in this book. Special thanks go out also to our other friends and colleagues at QVerity, including founding partner Bill Stanton, training specialist Jack Bowden, and marketing guru Bryan Stevenson.

Among the others who have touched this book with their extraordinary skills are those who read and re-read various iterations of the manuscript, including Debi Houston, Jim and Frances Winstead, Alex and Terri Reeves, Mike and Penny Houston, Casey and Debbie Houston, Philip and Rebecca Houston, Chris Houston, Beth Houston, Nick Dawson, Ardith Tennant, and Marcy Romary. Our agent, Paul Fedorko of N. S. Bienstock in New York, had the vision to see that everyone should have access to what he had experienced in one of our training sessions, and the acumen to guide us through the transformation of that experience into the framework for this book. The crew at St. Martin's Press could not have been more professional or easier to work with, and we are indebted to their talented copyeditors and designers. Our editor, Marc Resnick, is the best in the business—his flexibility and good nature were matched only by the brilliance of his editorial craftsmanship. The trust he readily placed in us is deeply appreciated.

PHIL HOUSTON'S PERSONAL ACKNOWLEDGMENTS

If the greatest deception in life is to believe that any significant accomplishment is solely one's own, then perhaps the greatest treasures in life are the people around us without whom any goal is only a dream. Coauthoring this book would not have been possible without the unwavering support of my wonderful and amazing family, which includes my wife, Debi; my sons, Phil Jr. and Chris; and my daughter, Beth. Without their love, support and understanding, I never would have been able to pursue the kind of career that enabled me to travel the world, and in turn to develop the techniques that we have captured in this book. Also, special thanks to my kids for allowing me to share their personal stories and vignettes to illustrate some of our techniques in the book.

While there are many people whose friendship and support I will always cherish, there are four former Agency colleagues worthy of special mention. These four colleagues and I formed our first commercial venture to provide training in the detection of deception. Without the hard work, entrepreneurial spirit and dedication of Bill Fairweather, Jack Bowden, Gary Baron, and a fourth colleague, who for the time being must go unnamed, this book might never have been written. I will be forever indebted to them. Their careers in the service of our country are worthy of books unto themselves.

The Central Intelligence Agency is, of course, the backdrop for all we have written, and I would be remiss if I did not say a

ACKNOWLEDGMENTS

few words about this remarkable organization. Having worked there for almost twenty-five years, I cannot imagine spending a career anywhere else. While it is essential that most of the Agency's work be conducted in secrecy, it is also somewhat disappointing that everyone in the country cannot witness first-hand the incredible accomplishments that are achieved every day by Agency employees around the world. There is simply no finer or more dedicated group of people in the world, who work not for recognition, but only for freedom.

MICHAEL FLOYD'S PERSONAL ACKNOWLEDGMENTS

I am blessed to have been raised by a village. That village is Columbus, Nebraska, a small farming community in our nation's heartland, filled with stout-hearted people who live by example and not by words. No one ever accomplishes anything in life without the help of others. Sadly, space does not allow me to honor the countless people who have profoundly touched my life along the way.

I wish to give special thanks to my teachers, coaches, friends, and neighbors. To my life-long friend and partner in shenanigans, Steve Anderson—thank you for always having my back. To my high school track and football coach, Ron Callan—thank you for your inspiration and example. To my swashbuckling and entrepreneurial army buddy, Frank Argenbright—thank you for encouraging me to pursue the deception-detection profession all those years ago. To my mentor, the late John E. Reid, who referred to me as the "bald-faced lad from Nebraska"—I hope our book makes you proud. To my law school professors, Paula Lustbader and David Boerner—thank you for giving me one of life's most important gifts: confidence in myself. To my beautiful sisters, Julie and Stephanie—thank you for your guidance, generosity, and humor. In memory of my parents, Bill and Wilma Floyd—I want to express my deepest thanks for their influence and unconditional love. Most importantly, thank you to my wife, Estelita—child, adolescent, and adult psychiatrist extraordinaire—for your encouragement, support, wisdom, spirituality, and love. You are my rock.

SUSAN CARNICERO'S PERSONAL ACKNOWLEDGMENTS

Like my coauthors, I am fortunate to have spent my life surrounded by wonderful friends and family who have provided great direction and support over the years. Heartfelt appreciation goes to my parents, Anna Marie and Jack Brenton and Cliff Muncy, who I'm sure at times questioned some of my decisions, but nonetheless offered unwavering support. I'm very grateful to my marvelous friends and mentors, Sheila Derryberry and Warren Hammer, who expected only the best from me, both personally and professionally, and in the process led me to believe in myself. Without them, my participation in the book project would not have been possible. Though there is no room to thank them all, there are many more friends who have been instrumental in my coauthorship of this book, whether it was through providing me with story fodder or simply supporting the idea, and to them I am grateful. A special thanks to Cindy and Steve Gensurowsky, with whom I have shared countless hours sitting on the deck, sharing stories similar to those in the book, and dissecting life in general. You have been my lifeline for so many years, and your friendship is the gift of a lifetime.

Finally, the greatest thanks must go to my children, Lauren and Nick, for allowing me to use stories about you, both in our training and in the book. Our frenetic lives are not always easy, but your love and support, as well as your senses of humor, make each day worth greeting. I am so proud of both of you, and I look forward to continuing the journey towards adulthood with you both. Now, go do your homework! Love you guys.

DON TENNANT'S PERSONAL ACKNOWLEDGMENTS

I have the immense good fortune of living on the grounds of Green Acre Bahá'í School in Eliot, Maine, where values like truthfulness form the foundation of the school's very existence. My wife, Ardith, is on the staff here, so I'm able to live and work in an environment that fosters a deep appreciation for the inherent nobility of mankind. It was a gift to be able to help write this book in a setting where our flaws as human beings are recognized as hurdles that face us all. So it's a good place to be if you find yourself writing about situations in which people are tested with the choice to be truthful or untruthful. There is no inclination to judge or to cast any stones, because there are routine reminders that we're all in this thing together, and that we all have work to do to get to where we need to be. I want to express my sincere gratitude to all of our friends here at Green Acre, and in the greater Eliot community, for that cherished gift, and for their encouragement and support along the way.

When I consider everything that has happened in my life, and everyone who played a role in making my involvement with this book possible, my thoughts keep going back to my family. My kids—Ardith (named after her grandma, making her the third in a row), Don (yes, our first two kids had our names–just let it go), Dan, and Shelly—have given me more than I could ever give them in ten lifetimes of being their Daddy. They each have qualities that I hope I have when I grow up. Finally, and most precious of all, my beloved wife taught me what it means to truly love someone, and to truly be loved by someone. She is, and will always be, my angel.

INTRODUCTION

Welcome to Our World

Imagine that it's the late afternoon of September 11, 2001.
Rescue crews are dealing with the unthinkable amid the massive heap of acrid rubble at Ground Zero in New York, where
the Twin Towers of the World Trade Center stood that morning. The wreckage of United Airlines Flight 93 has turned a
peaceful field near Shanksville, Pennsylvania, into a horrifying disaster site. The charred gash in the northwest face of the
Pentagon, just minutes up the George Washington Parkway
from where you and your colleagues are still coming to grips
with what has happened, is smoldering. The United States of
America is under attack.

You're not unlike the hundreds of millions of your fellow
citizens of America and the world who are trying to come to

grips with the same thing. Just about all the emotions are the same. The difference is that you're an officer with the Central Intelligence Agency, and you have unique skills that will be tapped to help determine the source of the attack, the nature of the immediate threat to the nation, and our country's best chances for preventing a recurrence. Welcome to our world.

The three of us came into this world from entirely different directions, and from vastly different backgrounds. The common denominator was the combination of a fascination with human nature, and a conviction that untruthfulness lies at the heart of all too many of the problems we face as individuals, as a nation, and as a global community.

Phil Houston was a career CIA officer, whose years of experience as an Agency polygraph examiner positioned him not only for senior-level assignments overseeing internal investigations and the security of CIA personnel and facilities, but for the creation of that unique skill set, borne of hundreds of interviews and noncoercive interrogations, that the country would be tapping at one of the most dire hours in its history. Michael Floyd's CIA service was preceded by a separate career as a private-sector polygraph expert. He provided training for polygraph examiners in the CIA and throughout the public and private sectors, and conducted polygraph examinations in hundreds of criminal investigations, many of them high-profile cases. Susan Carnicero, an expert in criminal psychology, was a CIA operative under deep cover before coming in from the cold and serving as a polygraph examiner and personnel screening specialist. Eventually, we shared an overarching, driving passion: to be able to know whether or not a person is telling the truth.

The deception-detection methodology we will share with you in this book has its roots in the polygraph-examination experience—an experience that can ascertain a person's truthfulness quite effectively when administered by a skilled examiner. Our methodology can be employed with a degree of effectiveness that equates to or even surpasses what is achieved by means of a polygraph.

Phil was the principal architect of the methodology, which was developed within the CIA for applications that were Agency-specific, and that cannot be shared here due to the need to protect CIA sources and methods. But its effectiveness became so quickly and widely recognized that the broader intelligence community and federal law enforcement agencies sought and received training in the methodology. The three of us have since worked together to further its development and to fine-tune it for a wider range of applications.

The event that cleared the way for us to share the methodology with you took place in 1996, when Phil and several of his colleagues in the CIA's Office of Security received the Agency's permission to provide the training to the private sector. While much of its application within the intelligence community was clearly classified, the methodology itself was determined to be unclassified, so there was no reason the training couldn't be made available to outside interests. Susan, who would become the lead instructor in the methodology within the Agency, joined the outside effort a short time later. Since then, the three of us have provided the training to hundreds of organizations, from Wall Street clients, corporate enterprises, and law firms, to nonprofits, academic institutions, and local law-enforcement agencies.

Still, we recognized that the applicability of the model is so universal that there remained a massive audience that we could never hope to reach through our training programs. So we decided that the next logical step was to introduce the model to people everywhere who could use it in everyday life—at work, at home, and at school. That's where you come in.

You, like everyone else, routinely have questions, the answers to which have a meaningful impact on your life. Is your boss being completely up front about those projections for the next two quarters and why it behooves everybody to stick around rather than bolt to a competitor? Is your significant other being straight with you about having done nothing more last night than hook up with a couple of friends for a drink? Is your child being honest when he assures you that he has never experimented with drugs? Other questions may be less personally consequential, but you still want the answers: Does that quarterback mean it this time when he says he's not coming back next season? Is that politician being truthful when she says she's not going to run for president?

Imagine that you were able to identify deception in response to these and the countless other questions like them that arise all around you every day—that you were successful in developing skills that take you to what we call the "spy-the-lie moment." Welcome to your new world.

1.

The Difficulty We Have in Calling Someone a Liar

People do not believe lies because they have to, but because they want to.

—Malcolm Muggeridge

It appeared that Phil had drawn the long straw that day. The foreign asset he was scheduled to meet at a downtown hotel in a country that can't be identified due to the sensitive nature of the CIA's work there had served the Agency well for twenty years, and his loyalty was thought to have been proven. The asset, whom we'll call "Omar," had been questioned by CIA personnel on numerable occasions over the years in debriefings and routine security interviews, and his credibility was reinforced with every encounter. Omar had earned his stripes as a trusted partner who was prepared to carry out the mission whenever he was called upon.

Phil and an Office of Security colleague had been dispatched from their home base at Langley a couple of weeks earlier to conduct routine interviews with key assets in several countries in the region. Just like the CIA employees themselves, these assets had to be regularly interviewed to ensure that they continued to meet the Agency's stringent security requirements. The work was interesting—it was always a welcome change to get out into the field—but grueling. These interviews could be extraordinarily intense and could go on for hours if an asset showed any sign of deception under questioning.

A stickler for doing his homework, Phil reviewed Omar's file like he was preparing to coach his beloved East Carolina University Pirates in a game against Virginia Tech. He studied accounts of Omar's past activities as if he were watching game film, trying to pick up any obscure detail or nuance that would help ensure a win. When he finally closed the file, he basked in his good fortune. This one was going to be easy. Omar was obviously squeaky clean.

Phil's colleague caught him at the door as he was leaving their secured location to conduct the interview with Omar.

"Hey, I guess you're not gonna be around to get some dinner later, huh?"

"Oh yeah, I will—this one's a piece of cake," Phil assured him. "I'll be there in two hours."

His colleague was clearly skeptical. "No way," he said.

"Look, I finally got lucky," Phil insisted. "I know I've had a ton of tough ones lately, but this one's different. This guy's been looked at by so many of our guys that there really just isn't anything to worry about. Two hours."

Phil headed for the prearranged site of the meeting, a guest room in a high-rise hotel in the middle of town. Just getting Omar to the hotel was a clandestine operation in itself, a carefully choreographed plan that had been carried out with exacting precision to protect Omar from discovery by hostile intelligence services. When Phil and Omar were securely settled in the designated room—a suite with a comfortable sitting area on one of the higher floors—the two engaged in cordial conversation, and then Phil got down to business.

Phil sat on the sofa, and invited Omar to have a seat in the adjacent easy chair. With hundreds of similar interviews under his belt, Phil had the drill thoroughly rehearsed. He was re-laxed, but businesslike, as he began to go through the prepared list of standard questions. Not surprisingly, Omar responded to them directly and comfortably—Phil could see that after twenty years Omar, too, knew the drill.

"You've worked for us for years," Phil acknowledged. "Have you ever worked for anybody else?"

It was an easygoing way of confronting this longtime, trusted asset with the question that had to be asked: Had he ever worked for the bad guys? What happened next stunned Phil.

Omar shifted in his seat, paused, and with visible discom-fort responded with a question: "Can I pray?"

Phil felt like a quarterback who'd gotten creamed from be-hind as he scrambled out of the pocket. *Whoa. Where did THAT come from?* He had absolutely no expectation of seeing that behavior from Omar. And yet there it was.

"Sure, no problem," Phil said, still recovering from the wal-lop. He expected Omar to bow his head for a few moments, and then proceed with his response. So what came next was even more puzzling.

Omar got up from the chair and went into the bathroom, and returned with a towel. Whatever this guy was doing, Phil was thinking, it wasn't good. And it simply didn't make any sense. Omar's unblemished record and Phil's certainty that he hadn't been lying in the interview to that point meant there had to be a reasonable explanation for Omar's actions.

Omar approached the window as Phil scrambled to make sense of what was happening. *What is this guy doing? Is he going to try to signal somebody with the towel? How bad is this going to get?* And then it dawned on him. Omar is Muslim. He was at the window to get his bearings so he could pray in the direc-tion of Mecca. Muslims pray at set times throughout the day, and maybe this was one of those times.

Sure enough, Omar carefully spread the towel on the floor to use it as a prayer rug, and prostrated himself on it. As Omar prayed, Phil's mind was whirling, and he began to second-guess himself. Had he said anything to offend Omar? Had he been disrespectful of Omar's faith? He couldn't help but hope that it was his handling of the interview, not Omar's actions, that were problematic. After all, Omar was a key asset of the local CIA operation. If Phil were to go back with the claim that a source who had been trusted for so many years and cleared by so many previous interviewers was bad, the head of the local operation was likely to want Phil's scalp, not Omar's. Beyond all that, Phil was getting hungry, and the dinner appointment he promised he would keep was approaching. No one wanted to believe that Omar was clean more than Phil did.

After praying for about ten minutes, Omar arose, folded the towel, and returned to his seat. As Phil gathered his thoughts to resume the interview, he recognized that he was being swayed by his own bias in wanting to believe Omar, rather than sticking to an objective assessment of Omar's behavior. There was only one thing to do: hit him with the question again.

The response was hardly what Phil was hoping for. Omar paused and shifted his feet uneasily. "Why are you asking me this?" he protested. "Is there a concern?"

If there wasn't before, there was now. Omar's verbal and nonverbal behavior in response to the question told Phil it was time to shift into elicitation mode. Calling upon his well-honed skills in nonconfrontational interrogation, Phil became something of a human GPS, navigating to a predetermined destination: a confession.

Phil reached his destination sooner than even he expected. In less than an hour, Omar admitted that he had been working for an enemy intelligence service for the full twenty years that he had served as a CIA asset.

Still, Phil's job wasn't over. Instead, it took an essential twist. Now he had to be assured that Omar was telling the truth when he claimed to have been working for the bad guys all those years. Remaining squarely in interrogation mode, Phil began asking questions to elicit information that would corroborate Omar's confession. With the truth he managed to conceal for two decades finally exposed, Omar recounted how for years he had to pretend to be a novice when he underwent CIA training—more often than not, he had already received the same training from the bad guys. He began to go into explicit detail about some of his successes against the Americans. One of his accomplishments was particularly chilling.

The individuals who hold the keys to the secrets of any CIA operation anywhere in the world are the communications officers. They are the ones who handle all the message traffic between their post, Langley, and other CIA posts worldwide. They have access to the CIA's ultrasensitive communications network and every classified document that's transmitted to or from their post. If hostile intelligence services see the personnel at a CIA post as a potential gold mine of information, the comms officers are the mother lode.

Omar, it turned out, had gotten disturbingly close to the communications personnel at the nearby CIA post. The location had two comms officers who shared a house and employed a servant from the local population. Omar had scored a major win by gaining eyes and ears inside the comms officers' residence: He recruited the servant.

That revelation came as another body blow to Phil, who was well aware of the damage that such a compromise could inflict. This time, the impact was swiftly moderated. Omar went on to confide in Phil that after only a couple of months, the servant abruptly and unexpectedly quit his job at the comms officers' home. When Omar went to his handler to deliver the bad news, the handler, a former competitive weight lifter, was so incensed that he picked up a chair and broke it with his bare hands. Omar told Phil he had no idea of the value the bad guys placed on having an asset within the comms officers' living quarters, and he began to fear for his own safety when the handler got in his face and began screaming uncontrollably at him.

Phil nodded attentively and compassionately as Omar unloaded it all. Inside, he was exhilarated. He had missed plenty of dinner appointments with far less consolation.

It was dawn when Phil wrapped up the interview. Omar went on his way, no doubt well aware that measures were firmly in place to ensure that the necessary follow-up on his case could proceed. Phil went back to the CIA facility and immediately cabled Langley. The revelation of Omar's duplicity was received with near disbelief. How could this have happened? How was Omar able to keep the masquerade intact all those years?

Phil was beginning to grasp the answers. Deception, he well knew, could be unyieldingly difficult to detect. He knew he had come perilously close to blowing it himself in that hotel suite with Omar. He recognized how much he wanted to believe this guy—he found himself looking for reasons to believe him, blaming himself for his insensitivity to Omar's religious beliefs and practices. It was only when he disciplined himself to adhere to a systematic, objective approach to the interview that he prevailed.

That systematic approach was crystallizing in Phil's mind. It was a work in progress, an amalgamation of the training he had received and the attention he gave to the behaviors he had observed in the course of conducting hundreds of interviews. He seemed to have a knack for assessing human behavior, and it was becoming more acute all the time. There was a gut feeling at work, yet it was more than that. There was a cognitive analysis going on, an almost imperceptible, subconscious cataloging of verbal and nonverbal behaviors exhibited in response to the questions Phil would ask. And those behaviors were beginning to coalesce into an approach to detecting deception that was proving to be extraordinarily effective. Phil was transforming his knack into a quantifiable, replicable set of skills. He had no way of knowing at the time that that transformation would ultimately lead to a methodology for distinguishing truth from deception that officers throughout intelligence and law enforcement communities, and ultimately people from all walks of life in the private sector, would be trained to use.

2.

Navigating the Deception Detection Obstacle Course

The greatest problem in communication is the illusion that it has been accomplished.

— *Daniel W. Davenport*

There is no such thing as a human lie detector. Let us be clear that we certainly don't think of ourselves that way. No individual on the planet can know beyond question whether what someone says is a lie, unless it's contrary to what that individual already knows to be true. If someone tells you he was an assistant coach with the Washington Redskins under head coach Mike Shanahan in 2008 and 2009, and you happen to know that Shanahan wasn't hired by the Redskins until 2010, you know that the person has told you a lie. If you don't know Mike Shanahan from Mike Ditka, and you have no clue who coaches the Redskins, you have no way of knowing at that moment whether the person is lying. Nothing in this book, or any other book, will change that.

What we can do, however, is give you some tools that have proven in countless situations to be remarkably effective at detecting lies, and we can show you how to use them. Think of those tools as the means of applying the systematic approach that Phil was developing in the course of conducting those hundreds of interviews and interrogations for the CIA—an approach that was ultimately molded into our deception detection methodology.

Before we get into the nitty-gritty of the methodology, it's important to understand that there are some formidable obstacles that get in the way of successfully detecting deception. Here are some that we've found to be especially challenging:

THE BELIEF THAT PEOPLE WILL NOT LIE TO YOU. This is the main obstacle that Phil had to deal with in his encounter with Omar, who had already been vetted and whose veracity and good standing were unquestioned when Phil interviewed him. In a more everyday setting, we think of this one as a social obstacle. In our society we operate with the belief that people are innocent until proven guilty, and with a mentality drilled into us since we were children that lying is one of the worst things you can do. Parents tell their kids that if they mess up, lying about it is ten times worse than whatever it was they did that they shouldn't have done in the first place. That's a powerful influence that can cause real discomfort when we're placed in a position of having to label someone as a liar, and we find ourselves wanting to believe people. The problem is that people *do* lie, and they lie a lot. Some behavioral research suggests that on average, we lie at least ten times in a twenty-four-hour period, including the so-called "white lies" that we tell in order to avoid hurt or conflict. So the psychologists will tell you that anyone will lie to you if he believes it's in his best interest to do so. What we would add is that he's more likely to lie to you if he believes he can get away with it.

Another factor that causes us to want to believe people is that most of us feel uncomfortable sitting in judgment of anyone else, and rightly so. We don't want to be casting any stones at anyone because we know that we're not in any position to do so. What we need to remember, however, is that the process of ascertaining the truth is not in itself a judgmental endeavor. In fact, if we allow any sort of judgment to creep into the process, we handicap ourselves because it distracts us from the systematic approach we need to take in order to find the truth. The three of us have absolutely no inclination toward or interest in sitting in judgment of anyone whose truthfulness we assess. Our sole aim in detecting deception is to deliver factual data to inform the decision-making process so that the best decision in any given situation can be made.

RELIANCE ON BEHAVIORAL MYTHS. There are a lot of behaviors that we've heard, that we've been told, and in some instances we've been taught, that are signs a person is or isn't being truthful. We have found, however, that there simply isn't a sufficient body of anecdotal or empirical evidence to support them, and that they're not nearly as reliable as the behaviors we will share with you. We would recommend, therefore, that they not be employed in a deception-detection scenario. We'll talk about some of these behaviors in chapter 12.

THE COMPLEXITIES OF COMMUNICATION. Perhaps you've never thought about it this way, but when you're trying to figure out whether a person is lying to you or telling you the truth, what you're analyzing is communication. The problem is that communication can be a very iffy proposition, for a couple of reasons.

First, due to the imprecision of language, we often hear a word and then put our own spin on it, and that interpretation is what guides our understanding of what's conveyed to us and how we act in response. The second issue is that words aren't all we have to deal with when we analyze communication—in fact, they don't even make up the lion's share. Research tells us that if we divide communication into two broad buckets—everything that's a word, or the verbals; and everything that's not a word, or the nonverbals—the majority of communication is nonverbal.

So why is that important relative to detecting deception? If we're trying to analyze what's being communicated to us, and the majority of communication is nonverbal, how much nonverbal training have we had? Possibly not all that much. On the other hand, we at least have the verbals under control, don't we? Maybe, maybe not. How many people would characterize their spouses as great listeners? The fact is, most of us aren't necessarily great communicators. That's an obstacle, which means we need to figure out how to manage some of the complexities associated with communication in order to successfully detect deception.

OUR INESCAPABLE BIASES. Although the word tends to have a negative connotation, "bias" is a simple fact of life, and it's not necessarily negative at all. We all have biases. If we have a favorite sports team, that's one of our biases. If we're not completely neutral about something, we're necessarily biased for or against it. The problem is that our biases have a huge impact on whether or not we believe someone. We don't have the luxury of checking our biases at the door when, for example, we need to interview a person. So we need some means of managing our biases so we don't even have to think about them during the interview.

Suppose you had been working on an actual case from the early 1990s in which the leader of a satanic cult in California was accused of molesting sixty child victims in the cult. One of these children, a soft-spoken thirteen-year-old girl, told investigators horrifying stories of what she and the other children had endured several years earlier at the hands of the cult leader. As might be expected, the cult leader denied it all, and there was no evidence to back up the sickening stories the girl recounted. Who was being truthful, the satanic cult leader or the young girl? No one who heard the girl's account had any doubt that she was telling the truth. Might bias have had something to do with their certainty?

Michael was called upon to interview the girl, and the model we will share with you made it possible for him to manage his bias during that interview. Michael discovered the truth: The girl acknowledged that her tale was an elaborate lie.

Susan once did a screening interview for a client who mentioned to her that a particular interviewee, whom we'll call "Mary," had been diagnosed with cancer. Like all of us whose lives have been touched by cancer, Susan could have been forgiven for allowing a heartfelt bias in favor of a cancer victim to influence her during the interview. By managing that bias, however, Susan found out quite a bit about Mary that shocked her prospective employer. During the course of that single interview, Susan learned that Mary was faking the cancer. Her parents had recently been killed in an automobile accident, which put a crimp in her lifestyle—she was on the verge of losing her yacht club privileges because the membership was in her parents' names. Mary discovered that the club allowed family members to keep their privileges for a year if there were extenuating circumstances, so she decided to tell the club manager that she had been diagnosed with cancer. Her plan worked, but since her best friend's parents belonged to the same club, she had to pretend to have cancer around that family, too. To top it off, her best friend's father felt bad for her, and gave her a job. "If I don't feel like working," Mary said to Susan, "I just tell them I have chemo that day." Suffice it to say, Mary didn't pass Susan's interview.

One more point to emphasize about bias: Never underestimate the power of its influence. No matter how good we think we are at this, if we don't manage our biases, we'll get beaten. Phil's two boys will tell you that growing up, they were guilty until proven innocent. His daughter Beth, on the other hand, was never guilty of anything. She was Daddy's little girl. Beth is as competitive as Phil and the boys are, so hopefully she wasn't keeping score.

THE "GLOBAL" INFLUENCE. Whether you realize it or not, whenever you've tried to read someone to determine whether or not he was being truthful, chances are you were using what's called "global behavior assessment." Global behavior assessment has a certain logic to it: You basically tell yourself, "I'm going to become a human vacuum cleaner, and I'm going to suck in as much information as I can so that I have the maximum amount of data possible at my disposal to make the best decision I can." As reasonable as it may sound, it's impossible to do. There is simply so much data coming at you, and so many tasks to perform in order to process that data, you just can't perform them all. It's like trying to get a drink of water from a fire hose. It can't be done. Beyond all of that, by using global behavior assessment, you put yourself in the position of having to guess at the significance of many of the behaviors you observe. For example, we often hear that if during an interview a person sits in a closed posture with his arms folded across his chest, that suggests he's withholding or hiding something. But what if the person just happens to be comfortable in that position? What if he's simply cold? We're just taking a shot in the dark at why he might be sitting that way, and that's hardly the most reliable way to collect accurate data.

What we need to do, then, is manage this flow of data coming at us by taking a more systematic approach that filters out all of that extraneous data. The model that we're going to share with you will enable you to do that.

Before we get to the model and a discussion of specific deceptive behaviors, there's one more thing that needs to be understood: Human behavior isn't necessarily logical, nor does it necessarily conform to our expectations. What each of us thinks of as logical is a reflection of our own beliefs, and of our own moral compass. A psychologist at the Agency hammered into us the fact that there's only a casual relationship between human behavior and logic. And we've found that to absolutely be the case.

Susan recalls having learned early on to expect the unexpected. Once, Susan, her toddler daughter, Lauren, and her friend Cindy went on vacation to Jamaica, and stayed at a family-owned cottage that was part of a hotel-resort property. A housekeeper and pool boy who had worked at the cottage for years were well known and trusted by the family, but on this trip, Susan also hired a nanny through the hotel to help take care of Lauren.

Susan and Cindy were so comfortable in the homey and familiar environment of the cottage that they thought nothing of leaving their money and valuables in their bedrooms rather than in a safe at the hotel. But after the first night at the cottage, Cindy mentioned to Susan that about forty dollars she had left on the dresser in her bedroom was gone.

Susan thought Cindy had probably just misplaced the money, but just as a precaution, they put all their cash in the hotel safe. On the day before their scheduled departure, Susan retrieved her cash from the safe, put it in her purse, and put the purse in a drawer in her dresser. The next morning she went for a final swim, and came back to find that her cash—about $1,200—was missing.

It didn't make any sense. The housekeeper and pool boy were like family, and the nanny, whom we'll call "Betty," was someone with whom Susan felt she could entrust the safety of her child. How could one of them have violated her trust?

Just prior to their vacation, Susan and Cindy had had their first exposure to our deception-detection model, and Susan decided to use it to try to make some sense of the situation. She went to the hotel manager to report the theft and to tell him that she needed to speak with Betty. The manager told Susan that it would be a fruitless effort. She would have no way of telling whether Betty took the money, he said. Betty would never admit to it, because it's just not a part of the Jamaican psyche to admit such a thing. Susan insisted, and the manager relented, though he did say that hitting Betty was not permissible. Fortunately, that wasn't part of Susan's plan.

Susan walked back to the cottage, eager to put the methodology she'd just learned into practice. She had her doubts about how effective she would be since she was so new at it, but she still wanted to give it a shot. When she got to the cottage, she called Betty into her bedroom and said she wanted to speak with her.

Betty came in, and Susan closed the door.

"I had quite a bit of money in here, and now it's missing," Susan said. "Betty, did you take the money?"

Betty took a step back and bumped into the dresser. "What money?" she asked.

"The money I had in my purse here in the dresser," Susan said.

Betty paused. "I've been taking care of Lauren!" she protested. "I haven't taken my eyes off of that child!"

Susan hesitated. Betty had indeed been taking remarkably good care of Lauren. Could she be telling the truth? Susan decided to press on.

"Betty, is there any reason the housekeeper and pool boy would say that they saw you in my purse?"

Betty shifted uneasily. She said nothing. Susan decided it was time to ask a presumptive question—one that presumes something related to the matter in question. In this case, it was the presumption that Betty had stolen the money. (We'll discuss presumptive questions in depth in chapter 10.)

"Betty, what did you do with the money?"

"I'm sorry about that," Betty replied.

Susan was stunned. "What?" she asked incredulously.

"I'm sorry about that," Betty said. She reached into her bra and pulled out the money.

What Susan was feeling bordered on astonishment. This wasn't at all what she had expected, especially after having spoken with the hotel manager. His logic about the Jamaican psyche was blown out of the water, and her own expectations about how relentless Betty would be in professing her innocence were shattered. This stuff actually worked. At that moment, Susan was hooked. She learned that day that human behavior doesn't always conform to what seems sensible to us, and that what seems sensible to us isn't necessarily valuable in evaluating how a person thinks or acts. She would go on to use that knowledge in much more serious situations with much more far-reaching implications.

Phil was already there. He had found that we often have certain expectations, so that, for example, we might look at a person whom we consider to be sophisticated and smart, and presume that there's no way such a person would exhibit blatantly deceptive behavior. Sometimes we even second-guess ourselves, because we think the person exhibiting that behavior must know and understand what he's doing, and what that behavior is telling us. But the simple fact is, people don't necessarily think about their behavior in a manner that seems logical to us. So regardless of how smart and sophisticated some people may be, they do exhibit deceptive behavior.

Phil once interviewed a foreign asset who had recently been recruited by the Agency, an erudite man with a Ph.D. and a strong background in academia. Phil asked him a standard question about whether he had ever worked for any other country's intelligence interests. The man's response could hardly have been more peculiar. He suddenly stood up, said, "No, sir," and sat back down. It was as if he was back in academia, answering a question posed by a teacher in the old-school days. Eventually, he admitted that he had been recruited by the Russians to work for the KGB.

If that one was odd, another case was considerably more extreme.

Phil was interviewing a foreign agent who had been suspected of engaging in activity that was harmful to U.S. interests. When Phil posed the "Did you do it?" question, the agent held his finger up and looked him straight in the eye.

"You know," the agent said, "I could have you killed." Apparently, he didn't like Phil's question.

"I'm sure you could," Phil said. And he went right back to the question. We'll explain why in chapter 6.

3.

The Methodology: It All Comes Down to This

Advances are made by answering questions.
Discoveries are made by questioning answers.

—Bernard Haisch

There was nothing accidental about the creation of the methodology we use to detect deception. If there was any serendipity involved, it lay in the fact that when Phil joined the CIA in 1978, he was assigned to the Office of Security. As you might expect, that's the organization responsible for ensuring the security of CIA facilities, personnel, and information worldwide. After six months on the night shift in the Security Duty Office at Langley and about a year in the Washington field office, Phil heard about the Agency's need to fill some openings in a different division within the Office of Security—the Polygraph Division. Eager to broaden his experience, he decided to give it a shot.

Unfortunately, he was shot down. The chief of the Polygraph Division felt that Phil was too young and inexperienced to be an effective polygraph examiner. This might have been the end of the story, had some other events not fallen into place. Not long after, the chief retired. With the demand for new polygraph examiners still high, George Macelinski, the Division's deputy chief, reached out to Phil to see if he was still interested.

By that time, Phil had begun to have second thoughts about the polygraph job, and felt it probably was for the best that he had been turned down. He wasn't at all sure that he was cut out for it. From his own experience of having been through a polygraph examination as part of the Agency application process, and the stories a lot of his colleagues had shared about their experiences in the hot seat, it seemed that an examiner's nature had to be defined by some degree of coldness or dispassion. After all, the stakes are sky high in the realm where these examiners hone their skills—with people's lives and our national security very much on the line—so Agency examinations are extremely serious business. Aside from that, any polygraph examination is an extraordinarily invasive procedure, and the examiner has to be equipped to handle situations that often subject people to intense emotional discomfort.

Phil simply didn't fit the cold, dispassionate mold. He was just a regular guy, a brand-new dad with a friendly, easygoing disposition who thought of himself as the nice-guy type. So when George approached him, Phil expressed his concerns. It didn't take long for George to allay them.

"That's exactly what we want," George said. He explained that Phil's personality type was the most effective in obtaining objective, balanced information, and in accurately assessing behavior. Being able to make the call that a person isn't lying is just as important as being able to make the call that he is, George said. The "nice-guy type" tends to have a sense of fairness, and to be able to manage his biases. That was all Phil needed to hear, and he was soon on his way to Chicago for six months of polygraph training under the tutelage of expert instructors, including Michael Floyd. The next fourteen years of his CIA career would be in the role of polygraph examiner.

Now, here's the thing about polygraph examinations. Just as there's no such thing as a human lie detector, neither is there any such thing as a mechanical lie detector. A polygraph machine doesn't detect lies. It detects physiological changes that occur in a person's body in response to a stimulus, the stimulus being a question posed by the polygraph examiner. Whether or not the anxiety associated with those changes is indicative of deception is an open question that must be answered by the analytical and human interaction skills of the polygraph examiner.

The pens on a polygraph chart record four physiological responses to the stimulus. There are two respiratory tracings, one cardiovascular activity tracing, and one galvanic skin response tracing, which records changes in skin moisture. The polygraph examiner will make precise annotations on the chart to indicate the points at which he begins and finishes asking a question, and the point at which the examinee provides his "yes" or "no" response.

At the conclusion of the polygraph examination, the examiner reviews the charts to analyze the degree of the examinee's physiological reaction in response to each question. Following well-defined rules of chart analysis, if the physiological indicators exhibited in response to a question meet the criteria for "deception indicated," the examiner will flag the question as being a problem area that warrants further attention.

It was in the course of just such a routine analysis that it hit Phil. If he'd ever had an epiphany, this was it. He would analyze these charts, making precise annotations that showed when he started asking a question, when he finished asking it, and when the subject provided his response. The sole reason for that was to establish a correlation between the question and any physiological reaction that followed. Phil asked himself why we aren't more disciplined when we conduct interviews and ask questions in our everyday encounters. What would be the result if we analyzed our conversations that way?

The answer is what has become our detection of deception methodology, or what we refer to simply as "the model." One of the beauties of the model lies in its simplicity. It has one strategic principle and two simple guidelines. The strategic principle is that if you want to know if someone is lying, you need to ignore, and thereby not process, truthful behavior. We'll delve into that seemingly paradoxical principle in the next chapter.

For now, let's focus on the two guidelines, which stem from Phil's "Aha! moment" when he was analyzing those polygraph charts. The two guidelines are *timing* and *clusters*. Although the concepts of timing and clusters were not new to the world of behavior assessment, no one had thought to meld those concepts into a codified behavior assessment model based upon the science of polygraph chart analysis.

Remember we said that the problem with global behavior assessment is that it puts us in the position of having to guess why a person is exhibiting a particular behavior. To make that leap from guessing to actual analysis, we need to focus on those behaviors that we can reasonably associate with a cause, the cause being the question. Think of analysis as identifying a cause, identifying the ramifications of that cause, and then exploring the relationship between the two. When we refer to timing, we begin with the question or statement that's the stimulus for the potentially deceptive behavior.

In order to determine whether a person is being untruthful, we need to look and listen for the first deceptive behavior to occur within the first five seconds after that stimulus is delivered. To understand why we set that span at five seconds and not, say, thirty seconds or sixty seconds, consider the fact that data from stenographers tells us that on average, we speak at a rate of 125 to 150 words per minute. Cognitive research, meanwhile, suggests that we think at least ten times faster than we speak. What that tells us is the further in time we get away from the stimulus, the higher the likelihood that the brain has gone on to thinking about something else. Our experience has shown that if we can identify the first deceptive behavior within that first five seconds, we can reasonably conclude that the behavior is directly associated with the stimulus.

Let's consider those deceptive behaviors. At any given moment in time, as human beings we tend to be either visually dominant or auditorily dominant—we're either more aware of and processing what we're seeing, or more aware of and processing what we're hearing. The problem with that goes back to what we said about communication being both verbal and nonverbal in nature, which means that deceptive behavior can come in either or both forms. How do we capture both at the same time?

The trick is to train our brains to go into what we call "L-squared mode"—we have to tell it to *look* and *listen* simultaneously. We have to say, "Brain, for the next few seconds, you're going to process in both the visual and auditory channels what's being communicated to me." Your brain will not like you for this. In fact, your brain will win the argument. After a period of time, your brain will say, "I've had enough," and it will default you to one or the other. But with practice, in those few moments following the stimulus you'll be able to condition your brain to go into L-squared mode. You'll be able to reliably collect and process the critical information you need to detect deception, and the volume of information will be higher than what the average person collects and processes.

The other guideline has to do with clusters of deceptive behavior. A cluster is defined simply as any combination of two or more deceptive indicators, which, you'll remember, can be either verbal or nonverbal. So a cluster might be one verbal and one nonverbal, or two nonverbals, or two verbals and one nonverbal, and so on.

What do you do if there's just a single deceptive behavior in response to the stimulus? You ignore it. There are a couple of reasons for that. First, we as individuals do a lot of things for different reasons. We have speech habits and patterns, and we have physical habits and patterns. They don't have any particular significance, they're just part of who we are. The process of filtering those out begins with the cluster rule.

Second, as you might intuitively expect, we have found that the higher the number of deceptive behaviors a person exhibits, the greater the likelihood of deception. As we said right up front, we can't become human lie detectors. But the simple fact remains that our confidence level rises in direct proportion to the number of behaviors we observe.

Now, let's meld the two guidelines. You ask your question, and you go immediately into L-squared mode, looking and listening for a cluster of two or more deceptive behaviors. Remember, the first deceptive behavior has to appear within five seconds of the stimulus. The cluster is comprised of that first behavior, be it verbal or nonverbal, and all verbal and nonverbal behaviors that follow it until the stream is broken by another stimulus or identifiable interruption. How long can the stream continue? We don't want to pick on politicians, but chances are we've all seen some long-winded responses in that realm that help provide the answer: pretty long.

Let's take a look at a couple of diagrams to illustrate the cluster rule. Think of this as a preview of some of the verbal and nonverbal behaviors we'll explain later in the book. There's no need to focus on the particular behaviors for now—just note that some are verbal, and some are nonverbal.

In Figure 1, we have a mother asking her daughter if she did her homework. We know that the daughter's response can be considered a cluster because it fulfills the requirements: There are two or more behaviors, and the first behavior begins within the first five seconds after the question. In fact, in this case we see that the daughter exhibits a verbal behavior even before her mom finishes asking the question. What we have is question recognition—the daughter has been through this before, and is likely thinking faster than the mom is speaking. She comprehends the question prior to its conclusion, and exhibits a verbal behavior in response. We count this one as part of the cluster.

Figure 1

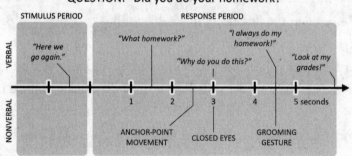

Illustration by Dan Tennant

Figure 2 is a much more serious scenario. Can we consider the response in this case a cluster? Yes, indeed—the first behavior occurs within five seconds of the question, and there are two or more behaviors. Our confidence level isn't as high in this case as it was in the case of Figure 1—the greater the number of behaviors, the greater our confidence level. However, as you can see, the number of behaviors in the cluster isn't necessarily a reflection of the seriousness of the deception.

Figure 2

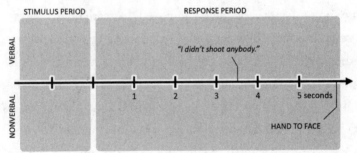

QUESTION: "Did you kill that police officer?"

Illustration by Dan Tennant

So, let's say all the conditions are met. You ask a question, and in response you get a cluster of deceptive behaviors, the first of which began within the first five seconds. Can you *definitively* conclude from that information that the person is lying to you? Nope. Remember, you're not a human lie detector. What you can conclude is that the question is a potential problem area, and that you have more work to do. There's a reason we refer to these behaviors as "indicators," not as "smoking guns."

But don't get us wrong. These indicators provide extremely valuable information, and by applying this stimulus-response model to their analysis, you'll find yourself experiencing the spy-the-lie moment and detecting deception with extraordinary effectiveness. One of the reasons for that is the surgical nature of the model's application.

When a surgeon removes a malignant tumor, he doesn't mark off a large area around the tumor and proceed to cut out that entire portion of the person's body in order to ensure that the tumor itself is completely removed. Instead, he makes precise cuts in very distinct areas, recognizing that just because other areas of the body are healthy doesn't mean there's no tumor to be cut out. If you think of deception as a malignancy, you need to have a surgical tool that allows you to identify it so you can leave all the other areas alone. You need to be able to isolate the malignancy so you can deal with it. Consider, for example, the case of the job applicant with a foot fetish.

Susan once conducted a screening interview with a man who was applying for a sensitive government position. Her final question was a catch-all question that was designed to identify potential problem areas that had not yet surfaced. (We'll discuss catch-all questions in chapter 10.)

"What haven't I asked you that you think I should know about that might be a concern?" Susan asked.

The applicant shifted uneasily. "What do you mean by things that might be a concern?"

That failure to understand a simple question is a deceptive behavior that we'll examine further in chapter 5. For now, what's important to appreciate is that what was of concern to the applicant didn't reside in the questions Susan had asked up to that point. She recognized from the response to the catch-all question that she had more work to do. Before long, she was able to isolate what it was that was causing the applicant's discomfort. He admitted that he had on a number of occasions put sleeping pills in his wife's drinks at night to make her pass out so he could satisfy his foot fetish. He had even tried to chloroform her on one occasion, but his wife awoke as he was putting the rag over her face.

When FBI agents approached the CIA operative at Dulles International Airport on November 16, 1996, it was the stuff of spy movies. But there was no director, no sound or lighting technicians, no cameramen, no actors. Unfortunately for the United States, it was the real thing. Harold James Nicholson, known to his CIA colleagues as "Jim," was arrested and charged with spying for the Russian Federation. He would later plead guilty, and would be sentenced to twenty-three years and seven months in prison. He would also hold the distinction of being the highest-ranking CIA officer ever to be convicted of espionage.

One of those colleagues who knew Nicholson as "Jim" was Phil. The two had met in the '80s, when Nicholson was posted overseas as a young case officer, and Phil, also a relatively new CIA officer, had done some work with him. Their paths crossed again in the mid-'90s, when Phil was serving as head of security at the CIA's primary training facility known as The Farm, and Nicholson was assigned as an instructor there. For two years they lived near each other, socialized at the same events, and took part in some of the same recreational activities. Their kids went to school together; Phil's son Philip and Nicholson's son Nathaniel for a brief period carpooled to football practice together.

Phil remembers Nicholson as being friendly and outgoing, but he also remembers not being totally surprised when the FBI came to him and briefed him on its suspicions about Nicholson. There just seemed to be something different about the divorced father of three, something odd that Phil couldn't put his finger on. Nathaniel was kind of reserved and intro-verted, but struck Phil as a very nice kid. So it came as more of a shock when the news broke in early 2009 that Nicholson, operating from prison, had recruited Nathaniel and was using him to travel around the world to collect payments from his Russian handlers. That treachery got Nicholson an additional eight years behind bars. Nathaniel managed to avoid prison by cooperating with authorities to build the case against his father.

Nicholson's recruitment by the Russians had come in the

wake of the arrest and conviction of Aldridge Ames, the CIA officer and Russian mole who had compromised more of our nation's intelligence assets than any spy in U.S. history. The Ames case was a wake-up call for the Agency, and it set in motion a security and counterintelligence training program—a refresher of sorts—that all CIA employees would be required to undergo. Phil was selected as an instructor to provide that training, and he and a second instructor conducted the sessions for all personnel at The Farm. That included Nicholson, who had been spying for the Russians the entire time he was working at the facility.

Phil recalls that he would end each training session with this statement, "If, by any chance, there is any one of you who is working for the bad guys, please rest assured that you will be caught." To this day, Phil wonders what went through Nicholson's mind when he heard those words.

The key takeaway from all of this is that deception happens, and that detecting it requires active employment of the model. There is nothing passive or automatic about it. Having knowledge of the model doesn't mean that you suddenly have a superpower that enables you to see deception wherever it exists. Phil never had a direct conversation with Nicholson about working for the bad guys. So, absent that conversation, and any reason to ask questions about working for the other side, Phil wasn't going to spot the deception, even though he had frequent, substantive contact with Nicholson.

So, unless you're in that behavior assessment mode, there's

nothing that will come to your aid to make deception apparent to you. In other words, the model is only good when you use it.

One final note about how we put the model into practice. When word of the effectiveness of the model began to spread through the CIA, a senior Agency officer came to Phil and said he wanted to see firsthand how it works. The senior officer chose to sit in on a screening interview that Phil conducted with a young man who was applying for a position as a contractor. As Phil proceeded with his questioning, he identified behaviors that led him to probe more deeply into certain areas to elicit more information. Before long, the applicant admitted to being a recreational drug user, and said he used marijuana and cocaine on a fairly regular basis. As the interview progressed, he admitted that he was also an occasional drug dealer. In fact, he said he had made a profit of about $1,500 on the sale of some coke just within the past several weeks. He went on to admit that he had stolen a stereo system worth about $500 from a local retailer, and that he had broken his girlfriend's collarbone during an argument about six months earlier.

When the thirty-minute interview ended and the applicant was leaving, he turned to Phil and asked, "When will I know if I've gotten the job?" Phil glanced over at the senior officer, who had an incredulous look on his face. Phil suppressed a grin. "It shouldn't be more than a couple of weeks," he said. "We'll be in touch."

What the senior officer observed was not only the effectiveness of the model in obtaining truthful information, but that it's implemented in a way that's totally nonconfrontational, with no one feeling belittled, and without putting the interviewer or his organization in harm's way. The idea is that when the individual walks out, he's given you what you wanted, and he feels good about what he's done, because he doesn't see you as an adversary. You've simply helped him to do the right thing, and he's maintained his dignity.

4.

The Deception Paradox: Ignoring the Truth in Order to Find the Truth

No mask like open truth to cover lies,
As to go naked is the best disguise.

—William Congreve

When Phil was serving as chief of security at The Farm, he was working at one of the most secure installations in the country, and it was his job to keep it that way. The fact that unauthorized access to the place could have devastating consequences for national security was only part of the problem. Ensuring that none of the people entrusted to work there had strayed from that essential trustworthiness was equally crucial.

So, on an otherwise routine day when a female employee came to him to report that forty dollars had been stolen from her purse, Phil knew he had a potentially monumental problem on his hands. If someone on the inside had indeed stolen the money, what else might that person be willing to steal? If there's one thing that's intolerable in a place where virtually every bit of information that's kept onsite is classified, it's a thief.

The woman explained that two 20-dollar bills had been taken from her purse when she was at lunch, and that only one person other than herself—an employee we'll call "Ronald"—had access to the room where she'd left her purse. Phil arranged for Ronald to meet him in his office. When Ronald arrived, he was as composed as anyone summoned to the office of the Chief of Security could be expected to be.

Friendly and cordial by nature, Phil had no inclination to present a stern or harsh demeanor, but there was no doubting that he had a serious matter to discuss. He invited Ronald to have a seat and wasted no time in getting to the point. With matter-of-fact directness, Phil related to Ronald what the female employee had reported to him. Ronald listened attentively. When Phil was finished, Ronald said nothing about what Phil had conveyed to him. Instead, he reached over and gently tugged on Phil's sleeve.

"Come out to the parking lot with me, Phil," Ronald said. "I need to show you something."

Phil had long since ceased to be surprised by anything a person confronted with an allegation might say or do in response, but this one seemed particularly odd.

"What do you want to show me, Ronald?"

"Just come with me, Phil. You'll see," Ronald replied.

Phil had no intention of leaving the office. Ronald repeated the request, but he could see it was futile. Finally, he told Phil what he wanted him to see.

"I wanted to show you what's inside the trunk of my car," Ronald said. "It's filled with Bibles. Every week I take them wherever they're needed on behalf of my church."

Phil had no doubt that Ronald was being truthful about having a trunk brimming with Bibles. But Phil knew that in order to convince his accuser, a deceptive person may respond to an allegation with a truthful statement, often one that casts himself in a highly favorable light. It's what we call a "convince vs. convey" situation—an attempt to convince the accuser of one's uprightness, of being the type of person who would never do anything like what he's been accused of doing, rather than to convey information that addresses the facts of the case.

Phil had seen and heard this sort of response in countless cases, and the red flag in this one couldn't have been waving any more conspicuously. If the truth had been on Ronald's side—if the facts had been his ally—he would have been adamant that he didn't take the woman's forty dollars, and everything he said would have focused on that. Phil knew he had to ignore Ronald's truthfulness about the Bibles in order to arrive at the truth about who stole the money. Calmly but unyieldingly, Phil pressed on with his questions. Less than ten minutes later, Ronald admitted to the theft.

———

Around the same time, when Michael was working as a polygraph expert prior to joining the CIA, he was called upon to interview a male student at a prestigious university. The student—let's call him "Anil"—was hardly a typical underclassman. A middle-aged man who had emigrated to the United States from East Asia, Anil already held a graduate degree in mechanical engineering, but he wanted to go to medical school. Anil was taking a biology class at the university in order to qualify.

Accomplished as he was as an engineer, Anil had failed two midterm exams in the biology class. In fact, he failed them dismally, and he desperately needed to ace the final. Anil arranged to be one of a handful of students who were to take a makeup exam several weeks after the original final exam took place. The average exam score was 99 correct out of 200 questions. Amazingly, Anil scored 184 correct.

Anil's score was brought to the attention of university officials, who had discovered that someone had posted the answers on a Web site before the makeup exam was administered. There appeared to be an explanation for this failing student's phenomenal performance on the final. Anil was formally accused of cheating.

Beyond the horror of the social stigma that suddenly enveloped him, the black mark could dash Anil's hopes of going to medical school. He adamantly denied the accusation, and he hired an attorney to clear his name. The attorney, convinced of Anil's innocence, in turn hired Michael to administer a polygraph examination to prove he was being truthful.

When Anil arrived for the test, Michael noticed that he was carrying what appeared to be a large photo album. After a cordial greeting, Anil seated himself and immediately steered the conversation to the album, which he opened to reveal pages of beautiful photos taken in his home country.

"This is my home," Anil said, pointing to photos of an ornate palace. "It's been featured in magazines." Michael looked at the photos intently, and commented politely on the beauty of the home. He nodded appreciatively as Anil continued to flip through the pages of the album, highlighting photos that had been taken of him with various dignitaries. Anil had no way of knowing what was really going through Michael's mind as he identified the dignitaries: "This guy's attorney is going to be very unhappy with what I'm going to have to tell him."

Anil's insistence that Michael see the photos before the polygraph exam began told Michael precisely the same thing that Ronald told Phil with the trunk full of Bibles: "I'm guilty as sin, but hopefully I can persuade you otherwise by showing you something that's truthful and that casts me in a halo-like light that will convince you that someone like me could never do what I'm being accused of doing."

Between that and the deceptive behaviors Anil exhibited in the pre-polygraph interview—behaviors that we'll discuss in the next chapter—Michael knew Anil was being deceptive well before he hooked him up to his polygraph machine, but the procedure was required to fulfill his obligation to the attorney. Sure enough, Anil failed the polygraph test, even more dismally than he had failed his biology midterms.

The idea here is that if you want to know if someone is lying, you need to ignore truthful behavior so that it's not processed. That seems counterintuitive to most people, and downright nonsensical to many. Yet it's one of the core principles underlying the model. And for good reason.

Let's say Phil has a deep admiration for people who devote themselves to the spiritual well-being of the community. If he hadn't been conditioned to ignore behavior that's truthful but doesn't address the issue of culpability in the matter at hand, might he have been swayed by Ronald's trunk-full-of-Bibles story? Likewise, suppose Michael is fascinated by East Asian culture, and has an abiding respect for people who demonstrate pride in their heritage. Might Anil's desire to share his photo album with Michael have influenced his perception of Anil's character and the likelihood that he would not only cheat on a test, but lie about having done so?

Ignoring truthful behavior helps us manage our biases, so we don't even have to think about them when the task at hand is detecting deception. Beyond that, it reduces—often dramatically—the amount of data we have to process in order to make a decision about a person's veracity. The more extraneous information that can be filtered out, the easier it is to spot behavior that's deceptive.

It's also important to note that behaviors that are associated with truthfulness can easily be replicated by deceptive people. Truthful responses tend to be direct and spontaneous, and a person who is deceptive is generally able to respond that way to many questions, especially if he's prepared for them. Similarly, a truthful person is typically alert, composed, and attentive. Yet, untruthful people can, to varying degrees, demonstrate that same behavior. The solution is simple: Ignore it. The chances are too high that it will be used as a weapon against you.

5.

What Deception Sounds Like

When people talk, listen completely.
Most people never listen.

—*Ernest Hemingway*

Anyone who has seen a courtroom drama on TV knows the oath that is administered when a witness is sworn in to testify: "Do you solemnly swear to tell the truth, the whole truth, and nothing but the truth, so help you God?" What many of us probably haven't thought much about is just how brilliant that simple twenty-word oath is. Its brilliance lies in its comprehensiveness: All the lies that have ever been told or ever will be told fall into three categories, or strategies: lies of commission, lies of omission, and lies of influence. And the oath covers all three.

"*. . . to tell the truth . . .*" covers lies of commission. These are the straightforward, bald-faced lies. In 2009, when former

South Carolina governor Mark Sanford said he was hiking the Appalachian Trail when he was actually hiking up the skirt of his mistress in Argentina, that was a lie of commission. Nothing fancy, just a flat-out lie.

"_. . . the whole truth . . ._" covers lies of omission. In this case, it's not what a person says, but rather what he _doesn't_ say, that constitutes the lie—a strategy that tends to be considerably more comfortable to carry out than telling a lie of commission. Let's say Sanford had had legitimate business in Argentina, independent of his dalliance. If he had said he was in Argentina on business, but left out the part about some of it being funny business with his mistress, that would be a lie of omission.

"_. . . and nothing but the truth . . ._" covers lies of influence. We'll be discussing this strategy extensively in the next chapter, because it's so powerful and because the average person tends not to recognize it. When people lie to you successfully, it's often because they say things that manage your perception of them as it relates to the issue at hand. Suppose that when confronted with the allegation that he had a mistress in Argentina, Sanford had responded, "I've been a happily married man for twenty years, and I'm a devoted father." In that case, the lie resides in the attempt to influence our perception rather than to convey truthful information.

These, then, are the strategies that underlie deceptive verbal behaviors. Identifying these behaviors has been a career-spanning endeavor, the fruit of an examination not only of how we were successful in detecting deception over the years, but in some cases, how we were beaten, or nearly beaten. Phil learned early on the value of the latter.

When his son Chris, now a law enforcement officer in North Carolina, was in elementary school, it seemed he was always getting in hot water for not doing his homework. Chris came home from school one day to find that his dad had taken the day off, and Phil went right for the jugular.

"Chris, do you have any homework?" he asked.

"We had a substitute today," Chris replied, and he bounded upstairs.

"Oh, okay," Phil said, and he went back to watching TV. A few minutes later, it dawned on him. Call it a delayed spy-the-lie moment. He could see the headline flashing across his brain: "Nine-Year-Old Beats CIA Interrogator." He called Chris back downstairs.

"Chris, how much homework do you have?" he asked.

After some foot-shuffling, Chris responded, "A lot."

"Why do you have a lot?" Phil persisted.

"Well, we had a substitute today," Chris explained, "and all she did was give us these worksheets, and anything we didn't finish in class we had to finish at home."

Phil was on a roll. "Do you have any to finish?"

"Yeah, a bunch of them," Chris replied.

"Okay," Phil said. "Go do your homework."

A lot crystallized in Phil's mind that day about how people lie. If the facts are not their ally, people have to say something that convinces you, and the best thing they can say is something that's true or irrefutable. In this case, Chris's response when Phil first asked him if he had any homework was absolutely true, and it played off of Phil's predisposition to believe him. After all, how many times have you had a substitute teacher in school when it was like a free day that day?

The example also illustrates the fact that most people simply aren't comfortable telling a bald-faced lie. It would have been much more difficult for Chris if he had to say, "No, I don't have any homework." So, rather than commit the act, he just avoided the whole situation by telling a lie of omission.

In Susan's household, it was her son Nick who helped her refine her parental deception-detection skills. Like a lot of preteen boys, Nick went through the stage when he considered taking showers and brushing his teeth to be a waste of time. He made the additional blunder of routinely lying about it. Susan would ask him if he brushed his teeth, or if he took a shower, and he would invariably say that he had. Like most moms, she knew better. Even if she hadn't been able to tell by his behavior that he was lying, Nick's body and breath aroma would give him away.

Nick would always seem confused by Susan's perception. You could tell he was thinking, "I've given this my best shot. How in the world does she know?" His curiosity finally compelled him to ask Susan how she knew that he wasn't brushing his teeth, and that he was just sticking his head under the water and not taking a shower.

"It's what I do for a living," she said. Nick looked at her with an air of defeat.

"You need a new job," he grumbled.

Many parents, particularly mothers, believe they have an innate ability, a basic instinct, when it comes to reading their kids. And indeed they do. Without even thinking about it, they find it easy to identify deviations in behavior patterns that raise their parental antennae. But consider how much better you would be with these additional behavioral analysis tools that make up the methodology at your disposal. Relying on your gut is fine when the matter at hand has to do with your child doing his homework or taking a shower or brushing his teeth. But when it comes to issues like drugs, sex, bullying and abuse, just going with what your gut tells you may not be your best option.

Let's delve into the deceptive verbal behaviors that people use when the facts aren't their ally.

FAILURE TO ANSWER. If you ask someone a question and he doesn't give you what you ask for, there's a reason for that. One possible reason is that the facts aren't on his side, and he's trying to figure out how to deal with that. Now, should you immediately conclude that the person is lying because he didn't give you what you asked for? Absolutely not. Always remember the cluster rule—we need more than just that single behavior. After all, there could be other explanations. Have you ever spoken with someone who just can't seem to get to the point? Or the person might not have understood the question, or thought he heard a different question?

DENIAL PROBLEMS. Closely related to the failure to answer is the absence of an explicit denial of something in your question that involves an act of wrongdoing, or has consequences associated with it. Let's look at an example of how this behavior is exhibited.

On June 25, 2004, Vice President Dick Cheney was interviewed by Neil Cavuto of Fox News, who asked the vice president about a recent exchange he'd had on the senate floor with Senator Patrick Leahy. According to several press reports, Cheney used the "F" word in the exchange, but the senate wasn't in session at the time, and there had been no acknowledgement from Cheney that he had indeed dropped the "F" bomb. Here's an excerpt from the transcript of that interview:

Cavuto: All right. Sir, a couple of little issues I want settled, or maybe to get the real skinny on. One was this blowout you had the other day with Senator Patrick Leahy of Vermont. What happened?

Cheney: Well, we . . . I guess you could say we had a little floor debate in the United States Senate.

Cavuto: I heard it was more than a debate.

Cheney: Well, it was—I expressed myself rather forcefully, felt better after I had done it.

Cavuto: All right. Now, did you use the "F" word?

Cheney: That's not the kind of language I usually use.

Cavuto: All right, because the reports were that you did.

Cheney: Yes, that's not the kind of language I ordinarily use. But . . .

Cavuto: What did you tell him?

Cheney: I expressed my dissatisfaction for Senator Leahy.

Cavuto: Over his comments about you and Halliburton?

Cheney: No. It was partly that. It was partly . . . also, it had to do with . . . he is the kind of individual who will make those kinds of charges and then come after you as though he's your best friend. And I expressed, in no uncertain terms, my views of the . . . of his conduct and walked away.

Let's stop it right there. What should we conclude from Cheney's remarks? He seemed to dismiss the mere suggestion that he would use such language, so it might have been easy for Cavuto to construe that as an implicit denial and move on, right? Fortunately, he pressed on:

Cavuto: Did you curse at him?

Cheney: Probably.

Cavuto: Do you have any regrets?

Cheney: No. I said it, and I felt that—
     [Cavuto interrupts]

So there we have it. If Cheney had not used the "F" word, he likely would have explicitly stated that fact immediately after Cavuto raised the issue. Instead, he sidestepped the question by saying that's not the kind of language he usually or ordinarily uses. He was given a golden opportunity to deny it, and he failed to do so. Three questions later, Cheney acknowledged that he "probably" cursed at Leahy (that's an exclusion qualifier, which we'll discuss later in this chapter), and one question after that he admitted, "I said it."

The first type of denial problem, then, is an outright failure to deny. Instead of failing to answer the question, the person might simply fail to convey any sort of denial at all. If, for example, you ask a person a yes-or-no question—"Did you do it?"—and the person does not respond with a "no" statement like "It was not me" or "I didn't do it," that's significant. When the truth isn't an ally, the person is psychologically inclined to respond with information he feels more comfortable conveying.

Denial problems can take a couple of other forms:

- **Nonspecific denial.** If the "no" statement is delivered in a way that's more of a general focus than a specific expression of denial of the matter at hand ("I didn't do anything," "I would never do something like that"), that's also significant. It's subtle, but if a person says he didn't do *anything*, psychologically he's letting himself off the hook so he doesn't have to tell the bald-faced lie, "I didn't do it." It's a nuance that's easily missed by an untrained ear.

- **Isolated delivery of denial.** If in response to a question about wrongdoing, a person gives you a "no" response, but buries it in a long-winded answer, that's important. If the percentage of the answer that relates to the denial is relatively small, that's a bad thing. Consider it a deceptive indicator.

RELUCTANCE OR REFUSAL TO ANSWER. Sometimes, we'll ask a person a question and he'll say something like, "I'm not sure I'm the right person to talk to." In some instances, it's because he doesn't want to be the right person to talk to—it's an easy dodge. Or he may express reluctance with a response like, "Gee, I'm not sure I can answer that." Of course, these responses could be legitimate, so remember that you have to adhere to that cluster rule.

REPEATING THE QUESTION. Why might a deceptive person repeat a question? We think of it as buying time, and ultimately that's the goal. But what's happening, according to behavioral psychologists, is he's probably trying to fill in what would otherwise appear to be a very awkward moment of silence. Silence in response to a question is almost universally perceived as deceptive. So rather than just sit there in stone silence with a blank look on his face, he'll repeat the question to give himself time to think. What's interesting about this is that while it might take only two to three seconds to repeat the question, let's do the math. If a person thinks ten times faster than he speaks, he's just bought himself twenty to thirty seconds' worth of what he hopes will be good response material. As always, it's important to remember the cluster rule here. There are perfectly legitimate reasons to repeat a question— perhaps the person didn't hear it, or wants to ensure he understands it. And sometimes, it's just a habit.

NONANSWER STATEMENTS. The psychology behind nonanswer statements is much the same as that associated with repeating the question—avoiding that awkward silence and buying time to figure out how to respond. These are things that people say that don't provide what you ask for: "That's a good question," or "I'm glad you asked that." Sometimes, these can provide you with useful information. We often hear the nonanswer statement, "I knew you were going to ask me that." Why is that statement made in response to this particular question? Without realizing it, the person may be cluing us in on what he's thinking or worried about.

> **NONANSWER STATEMENTS**
>
> "That's a good question."
>
> "I'm glad you asked that."
>
> "I knew you were going to ask me that."
>
> "That's a legitimate concern."

INCONSISTENT STATEMENTS. "It is not without good reason said, that he who has not good memory should never take upon him the trade of lying." So said Michel Eyquem de Montaigne, who well knew that keeping your story straight when the truth isn't your ally is a formidable task. When a person makes a statement about an issue of interest to you, and subsequently makes a statement that's not consistent with what she said previously, and she doesn't explain why the story has changed, that is significant.

Tea Party member and former U.S. Senate candidate Christine O'Donnell appeared on CNN's *Piers Morgan Tonight* on

August 17, 2011, to promote her book, *Troublemaker: Let's Do What It Takes to Make America Great Again*. O'Donnell ultimately walked out before the interview was over because there were only certain parts of her book that she wanted to talk about, and Morgan refused to restrict his questioning to those parts. Here's a short excerpt from the exchange:

Morgan: So would you agree with Michele Bachmann that we should maybe [reinstate] Don't Ask Don't Tell, we should restore that?

O'Donnell: (laughs) I'm not talking about policies. I'm not running for office. Ask Michele Bachmann what she thinks. Ask the candidates who are running for office what they think.

Morgan: Why are you being so weird about this?

O'Donnell: I'm not being weird about this, Piers. I'm not running for office, I'm not promoting a legislative agenda. I'm promoting the policies that I lay out in the book that are mostly fiscal, that are mostly constitutional.

Within the span of two responses, then, O'Donnell said she was "not talking about policies" because she was "not running for office," and then said, "I'm promoting the policies

WHAT DECEPTION SOUNDS LIKE

that I lay out in the book that are mostly fiscal, that are mostly constitutional." She clearly couldn't have it both ways, and became entangled in a web from which she couldn't extricate herself without simply walking out. We'll look at a strategy for handling inconsistent statements in chapter 11.

We're going to delve into this particular interview more extensively in chapter 7, where we'll look at attack behavior, the next deceptive indicator on our list.

GOING INTO ATTACK MODE. Being backed into a corner by the facts of a situation can put a lot of strain on a deceptive person, and can compel him to go on the attack. This might take the form of an attempt to impeach your credibility or competence, with questions like, "How long have you been doing this job?" or "Do you know anything about our organization?" or "Why are you wasting my time with this stuff?" What he's trying to do is to get you to back off, to start questioning yourself on whether you're going down the right path. Kids will often give this a shot when confronted by their parents. Questions like, "Why do you always pick on me?" and "Why don't you trust me?" fall into this category.

INAPPROPRIATE QUESTIONS. Some schools of thought suggest that answering a question with a question is deceptive, but we would say that's not necessarily the case. What concerns us is when we ask a question, and the response is a question that doesn't directly relate to the question we asked.

63

Phil recalls taking part in an investigation involving a missing laptop computer. He interviewed a number of individuals who had access to the location it was missing from, and asked each person, "Is there any reason that when we locate the laptop, it will have your fingerprints on it?" Some of the people who were interviewed responded with questions like, "Whose computer was it?" or "What office did it come from?"—perfectly sensible, appropriate questions. But one young man, after a long pause, responded, "How much did it cost?" The question had no connection to what was asked, but he probably had a good reason for asking it: Was he looking at a misdemeanor or a felony?

OVERLY SPECIFIC ANSWERS. Deceptive people might be overly specific in two ways, and they're almost polar opposites. One way is they will answer a question too technically, or too narrowly. We recall analyzing an interview with a CEO who was asked about his sales that quarter. "I'm glad you asked that," the CEO responded. "Our domestic sales are up higher than we expected." As it turned out, domestic sales accounted for only about 10 percent of his company's revenue. Three weeks later, the company announced its earnings, and its performance was down markedly from the previous quarter. Global sales had tanked.

Then there's the famous 1992 interview of then-governor Bill Clinton by Steve Kroft of 60 *Minutes*. "[Gennifer Flowers] is alleging and has described in some detail in the supermarket tabloid what she calls a twelve-year affair with you," Kroft said. Clinton's response: "That allegation is false." Technically, he was correct. According to Flowers, the affair lasted eleven and a half years.

In addition to being overly specific by limiting the scope of the response, deceptive people might go to the other extreme of overspecificity and inundate you with detailed information in response to your question. Why would they do that? Remember the deceptive strategy of influence that people use to manage your perception of them? That often takes the form of providing you with more information than you asked for in order to create a halo effect. When Phil ran the internal affairs operation within the CIA, he required all of his investigators to ask employees being interviewed, "What do you do here at the Agency? What's your job?" Obviously, the investigators wouldn't have gone into the interview without knowing that. The purpose was something of a test. We found that truthful people tended to respond succinctly with a job title: "I'm a case officer," or "I'm an analyst." Deceptive people tended to provide a job description, offering specific information intended to manage the investigator's perception of them. What's interesting is that everything they said was the truth. But the purpose was to create that halo effect.

INAPPROPRIATE LEVEL OF POLITENESS. We're certainly not at all suspicious of someone who's just a nice person. But if, in response to a question, a person suddenly increases the level of nicety, that's significant. Perhaps the person says, "Yes, ma'am" in that particular response, but at no other time in the interview. Or a compliment might be injected during the response: "That's a great tie, by the way." The idea here is that the more we like someone, the more we're inclined to believe him and to shy away from confrontation. The person is using politeness as a means of promoting his likability.

INAPPROPRIATE LEVEL OF CONCERN. If the facts are not a person's ally, he's put into a hole from which he needs to try to extricate himself. A person in this position doesn't have much going for him, so he might resort to a strategy of attempting to diminish the importance of the issue. Typically, he'll focus on either the issue or the process, and try to equalize the exchange by doing the questioning: "Why is this such a big deal?" or "Why is everybody worried about that?" The person might even attempt to joke about the issue, which can be especially inappropriate.

PROCESS OR PROCEDURAL COMPLAINTS. Sometimes, a person won't necessarily go on the attack, but will still attempt to play offense rather than defense by taking issue with the proceedings. Questions like "Why are you asking me?" or "How long is this going to take?" fall into this category. They may be a delaying tactic, similar to repeating the question or making non-answer statements, or they may be an attempt at deflection in the hope of steering the proceedings down a different path.

FAILURE TO UNDERSTAND A SIMPLE QUESTION. When you ask a question, you often use certain words or phrases to establish boundaries that define the scope or magnitude of the question. If that particular wording traps the person, one strategy he might employ is to get you to change your phrasing or terminology. The aim is to shrink the scope or magnitude of the question, to give him just enough wiggle room to answer it to your satisfaction and to his. Perhaps the best-known example of this is the testimony of Bill Clinton before the independent counsel in the Monica Lewinsky case in August 1997. During the proceedings, there was a reference to a statement that had been made by Clinton's attorney: "Counsel is fully aware that Ms. Lewinsky has filed, has an affidavit which they are in possession of saying that there is absolutely no sex of any kind in any manner, shape, or form, with President Clinton." Clinton was asked whether that was a false statement. His famous response was, "It depends on what the meaning of the word 'is' is. If 'is' means is and never has been, that is one thing. If it means there is none, that was a completely true statement." Clinton was trapped by the magnitude of the statement under question, so he was forced to try to shrink the scope of it so he could answer truthfully.

REFERRAL STATEMENTS. Sometimes in response to a question, a deceptive person will refer to having previously answered the question. This might take the form of such statements as, "I would refer you to my earlier statement when I said . . ." or

"As I told the last guy . . ." or "As we have repeatedly stated in our corporate filings . . ." The idea here is to build credibility. It's a subtle tactic, but much more powerful than most people realize. We may not be convinced that the person is being truthful, but repetition is a psychological tool that often can make us more open to that possibility than we otherwise would have been.

Suppose you're at some no-name restaurant in the middle of nowhere with a friend, and she leaves to use the restroom. She comes back with an astonished look on her face.

"You're not going to believe this," she says, "but in that other room there's a table with every amazing guy you can think of!" She starts rattling off names: Johnny Depp, Gordon Ramsay, Jamie Foxx, Matt Damon, Matthew McConaughey, David Beckham, Leonardo DiCaprio, Brad Pitt, Christian Bale, Denzel Washington, George Clooney, Ryan Reynolds, Hugh Jackman, Steven Tyler, Will Smith, Pierce Brosnan . . .

"Yeah, right," you say.

"No, I mean it!" she insists. "They're out there! I saw them!"

You don't know if your friend is hallucinating or what, but you do know that there's just no way all of those guys are in the next room. You tell your friend that she may want to push her wineglass away.

"Look, I'm telling you," she says. "They're here. In that room. I have no idea why, but they're here."

Now you're beginning to wonder. As certain as you are that those guys simply aren't in that next room, you find yourself picturing them all at a table.

"Go look!" your friend says.

Finally, you give in. You get up and go look.

You've just been acquainted with the power of referral statements. Sheer repetition got the better of you. In many situations, making a claim one time doesn't have much of an impact. But each subsequent time the claim is made, it diminishes our resistance or disbelief, to the point where the door is opened to the possibility that the claim actually has credibility. Remember what Franklin D. Roosevelt said in 1939: "Repetition does not transform a lie into a truth."

INVOKING RELIGION. When a person brings God into the equation, he's engaging in an extreme form of what psychologists call "dressing up the lie," and it can be very effective. After all, what do you have in your briefcase that tops God? So, you need to recognize responses that include such phrases as "I swear to God" or "As God is my witness" for what they may well be: an attempt to dress up a lie in its Sunday best before presenting it to you.

> **INVOKING RELIGION**
>
> "I swear to God . . ."
>
> "As Allah is my witness . . ."
>
> "I swear on a stack of Bibles . . ."
>
> "God knows I'm telling the truth."

SELECTIVE MEMORY. When a person says, "I don't remember," that's a difficult statement to refute without some definitive, tangible evidence. It's a psychological alibi, and it's a hard alibi to crack. Another problem with selective memory is that it can easily be legitimate. Suppose you ask the CEO of a corporation of twenty-five thousand people, "Has anyone in your company committed fraud in the last twelve months?" If he responds with a resolute "No," that would be somewhat odd, because he probably would have no way of really knowing that. A more reasonable response would be, "Not to my knowledge," a response that in other situations could raise a red flag. If you had asked the CEO if he had engaged in any fraudulent activity in the last twelve months and you got that response, you'd clearly have a situation on your hands that you'd need to pursue. So, context is especially important when identifying this particular behavior.

> **SELECTIVE MEMORY**
> _____
>
> "Not that I recall . . ."
>
> "To the best of my knowledge . . ."
>
> "Not that I'm aware of . . ."
>
> "As far as I know . . ."

QUALIFIERS. There are two types of qualifiers that are potential deceptive indicators: exclusion qualifiers and perception qualifiers. Exclusion qualifiers enable people who want to withhold certain information to answer your question truthfully without releasing that information. Examples of qualifiers of this type include "basically," "for the most part," "fundamentally," "probably," and "most often." Perception qualifiers are used to enhance credibility: "frankly," "to be perfectly honest," and "candidly" are examples. Keep in mind that we all have speech habits and patterns that can account for the presence of these qualifiers, so again, remember the cluster rule. Also, we don't count each qualifier as a separate indicator. Consider the use of multiple qualifiers in response to a question as one indicator. There can be a lot of them in a single response. We'll examine a strategy for handling exclusion qualifiers in chapter 11.

EXCLUSION QUALIFIERS
"Not really . . ."
"Fundamentally . . ."
"Basically . . ."
"For the most part . . ."
"Probably . . ."
"Usually . . ."
"Possibly . . ."
"Most often . . ."

Michael once worked on a case involving a young woman who was employed as a bookkeeper for a small business. She was alleged to have stolen more than $7,500 by making out company checks naming herself as the payee, and using the rubber stamp of the owner's signature to sign them. When confronted with the allegation, she claimed that the owner had approved these payments in return for her silence about keeping two sets of books in order to skirt some tax liability. The owner denied that and reported her to the police.

Here's an excerpt from the transcript of Michael's interview with her:

PERCEPTION QUALIFIERS
"Frankly . . ."
"To tell you the truth . . ."
"Honestly . . ."
"To be perfectly honest . . ."
"Candidly . . ."
"Truthfully . . ."

Michael: Tell me about the part where he [the owner] said, "Now that you know [about the two sets of books], I'll take care of you so that you keep your mouth shut."

Bookkeeper: Well, he basically told me that he would pay me extra, you know, points or whatever. Basically, we didn't go into an extensive conversation, basically."

She was clearly making the story up as she went along, and she eventually confessed. At the time, she was about a month from satisfying a lengthy probation period on an unrelated felony. Now she was basically looking at prison time, basically.

CONVINCING STATEMENTS. Lies of influence, the category of lies that we spoke about in the opening of this chapter as being especially powerful, occur in the form of what we call "convincing statements." This behavior is so powerful that it warrants a more in-depth discussion. We'll do that in the next chapter.

6.

The Most Powerful Lies

Let your lie be even more logical than the truth itself,
So the weary travelers may find repose.

— Ceslaw Milosz

Like everyone in this business, we've dealt with our share of gut-wrenching cases. It's probably safe to say that none has been more gut-wrenching than the case of a man we'll call "Oscar," a U.S. government employee who was in a senior position as a GS-15. Oscar was under investigation for child molestation, and Phil was called upon to interview him.

When Phil asked Oscar if he was sexually involved with the kids, Oscar scowled at him. He wagged his finger and began to speak:

"Young man, I would never do that," Oscar seethed. "That would be perverted, and I am not a pervert."

Phil was unfazed. His response was delivered with engaging calm.

"Listen," Phil said, "I happen to have two little boys of my own. Quite frankly, if I thought you were a pervert, I don't think I could stay in the same room with you."

Oscar looked puzzled. He clearly didn't expect that reaction. He expected a fight or a debate, and instead what he got was agreement. Phil immediately went back to the line of questioning.

"Now, when was the last time you were alone with these kids?"

Oscar eventually admitted that he had molested hundreds of children. When Phil asked him where he would go to find the children, Oscar's response was chilling. He said his favorite place to go was a popular pizza-and-arcade chain that catered to kids.

When Oscar responded to Phil by saying that he would never do that, that child molestation is perverted and that he wasn't a pervert, he was employing convincing statements. If a person is asked a question and is unable to respond with the facts because the facts are not his ally, he is very likely to respond with these statements, which are designed to convince the questioner of something, rather than to convey truthful information.

Suppose someone asked you, "Did you take the missing money?" Since you're honest and didn't take any money, your most likely response would be, "No!" The reason is that's the single fact that's most important to you to get across. The guilty person may or may not deliver the "no," but the discomfort of the facts not being his ally will likely compel him to convey other information to convince you. "I would never do that," he might say. "That would be dishonest, and I'm not that kind of person," or "Ask anybody around here, look at my record," or "I have a good reputation," or "You think I would jeopardize my job by doing that?"

You may be thinking that this all seems rather obvious—that such behavior would raise a red flag that would be hard to miss. We can assure you, however, that unless you're in L-squared mode and are employing the model, you'll be vulnerable to these convincing statements, regardless of your background. The reason is simply that they're so, well, *convincing*. They tend to be perfectly reasonable, and they can be very difficult to catch simply because they make so much sense. You'll hear one, and you might think, "That sounds like something I would say myself if I were asked the same question." That might well be, but the difference is there would very likely be no more than one such statement, and there would be

NEUTRALIZE CONVINCING STATEMENTS

The way to combat convincing statements is to neutralize them—to render them ineffective by acknowledging or agreeing with them. This, of course, needs to be distinguished from agreeing with the action. In the Susan Smith example, (see p. 77), it would sound something like this: "Susan, I know you love your kids. I think that's evident to everybody." She might think for a fleeting moment, "I have them." But the next step is to stay on point and keep right on going in the original direction: "Susan, we want to talk to you now about what really happened. We want to go over your story again."

The message that's delivered is this: "We asked you a question. We heard what you said, and what you said had no impact on where we're going with this conversation." The beauty of it is you deliver that message below the radar. Above the radar would be, "Wait a minute, Susan, I don't believe you. I think you're lying through your teeth." That triggers defenses, and the person shuts down. Our job is to get her to open up to us. This tactic is enormously powerful and effective, whether a parent is speaking with a child, an employer is speaking with an employee, or a CIA officer is speaking with a terrorist.

more to your response, including a straightforward statement that you didn't do it. The deceptive person will often give you a string of convincing statements, because he has no choice. He has no facts that are his friend.

Let's look at a couple of examples of this behavior. Several years ago, Phil was conducting training for a group of law enforcement officers, and was discussing convincing statements when he noticed two officers chuckling in the back of the room. We tend to have a lot of fun in these classes, so Phil stopped midsentence, and with feigned schoolmarmlike indignation, he asked the two officers if they'd care to share what was so funny with the rest of the class. One of the officers explained that a colleague of theirs who was also in the class had been investigating a theft case in their town. A woman reported that a maintenance man had repaired a leaky pipe in her apartment while she was at work, and when she came home that day, she found that some of her jewelry was missing. The officer investigating the case interviewed

THE MOST POWERFUL LIES

everyone who had access to the apartment, including the maintenance man. When asked if he had taken the jewelry, this was his reply:

"I've been doing this for twenty years and I'm close to retirement. Why would I risk my pension for some stupid piece of jewelry?"

The two officers who had been chuckling said their buddy, the investigating officer, found that response so sensible that he no longer considered the maintenance man a suspect. Phil turned to the investigating officer.

"What do you think now?" Phil asked.

"I think I'll be talking to a maintenance man tomorrow," the officer replied.

Around the same time, we were providing training for the South Carolina Law Enforcement Division. One of the officers in the class happened to be from the small town of Union, South Carolina, whose most famous—or, more accurately, infamous—citizen is Susan Smith. Perhaps you recall the tragic 1994 homicide case in which Ms. Smith drowned her two young sons by letting her car roll

A TIP FOR PARENTS

If you're a parent, and the time has come for you to speak to your child about drug use, bear in mind that you must go into L-squared mode when you talk to your child, and be especially alert for convincing statements. Our experience has shown that teens who have experimented with drugs, when confronted by their parents, tend to rely heavily on convincing statements. If your child has not experimented with drugs, his likely response to your question will be something like "Absolutely not!" or "No way!"

Kids who have used drugs are unlikely to deny it. Instead, they typically rely on convincing statements such as:

into a lake with the boys strapped inside. She initially claimed a man had hijacked her car, but confessed to the crime nine days later.

During a break in the training session following our discussion of convincing statements, the officer, who was familiar with the investigation, came up to us. "For the first time," he said, "I think I understand how she successfully misled the investigators in that first interview." The officer said that when Ms. Smith was asked if she had anything to do with the disappearance of her children, her response was, "I love my children. Why would I do anything to hurt my kids? I would never hurt my kids." The officer said that at that point, the investigators, despite being seasoned professionals, believed she had nothing to do with it.

Those three convincing statements were tremendously effective, for three reasons. First, like all convincing statements, they were true or irrefutable. When she said, "I love my children," that was probably true on some level. When she said, "I would never hurt my kids,"

- "I can't believe you would think I would do that!"

- "I've never given you any reason to think that!"

- "Why don't you trust me?"

- "You're accusing me just because Josh got caught and Josh is my friend!"

You'll find a list of suggested questions to ask your child about drug use in Appendix I.

that was heartbreakingly untrue. But at the time she made it, it was irrefutable.

Second, convincing statements usually incorporate emotion. In this case, the officer said that when Ms. Smith made those statements, the investigators could see tears welling up in her eyes—the emotion is what expresses the conviction. Emotion in and of itself isn't necessarily truthful or deceptive. But untruthful people use it to enhance the deception.

The third factor is that the statements were consistent with the investigators' bias. "In our experience, moms just don't kill their kids," the officer told us. "And they darn sure don't do it in Union, South Carolina." That was interesting.

"Where do moms kill their kids?" Phil asked.

> ## CONVINCING STATEMENTS
>
> "No one would ever question my honesty."
>
> "I have a great reputation."
>
> "I'm an honest person."
>
> "My word is my bond."
>
> "It's not in my nature to do something like that."
>
> "I always try to do the right thing."
>
> "I would never jeopardize my job by doing something like that."
>
> "How could you even think I could be involved in something this serious?"
>
> "I have worked here for over twenty years."
>
> "I love you, I would never do anything to hurt you."

"Well, you know," the officer responded, "New York, L.A., Chicago." Even police officers can make a shaky generalization that the rest of us might also find ourselves making.

Unlike qualifiers, we consider each convincing statement as a separate deceptive indicator. So, two convincing statements constitute a cluster. They're *that* powerful.

7 ·

The Wrath of the Liar

No man lies so boldly as the man who is indignant.
—*Friedrich Nietzche*

In a federal courthouse in Houston on April 10, 2006, Jeffrey Skilling, the former CEO of Enron Corporation, took the witness stand at his own trial. He was charged with conspiracy, securities fraud, insider trading, and making false statements to auditors in the wake of the spectacular collapse of the now-defunct energy services company, and he took the stand to profess his innocence.

Skilling raised his right hand as the court clerk administered the oath: "Do you solemnly swear to tell the truth, the whole truth, and nothing but the truth, so help you God?"

"I do," Skilling replied, and he took his seat. Think back to chapter 5, and the all-encompassing nature of that oath, how it covers every type of lie Skilling could conceivably tell—lies of commission, lies of omission, and lies of influence. It's fascinating to consider what must have been going through Skilling's mind as he took that oath. Did he feel boxed in, or cornered, because the facts weren't his ally and the stakes were so enormous? Was that what caused him to lash out at those he blamed for his predicament?

"The witch hunt started," Skilling told the jurors. "People lost money. People lost jobs. The easiest thing to do is look for witches." The jury apparently wasn't swayed. Forty-five days later, it returned a verdict of guilty on one count of conspiracy, one count of insider trading, five counts of making false statements to auditors, and twelve counts of securities fraud. Skilling was sentenced to twenty-four years and four months in prison, and fined $45 million.

Five years before Skilling took the stand that day, he was already showing signs of feeling cornered. In a conference call with analysts and reporters on April 17, 2001, Richard Grubman, managing director of Highfields Capital Management in Boston, challenged Skilling over Enron's refusal to release its balance sheet along with its earnings statement.

"You're the only financial institution that can't produce a balance sheet or cash flow statement with their earnings," Grubman said.

"Well, thank you very much," Skilling replied. "We appreciate it. Asshole."

No doubt, there was much going through Skilling's mind

that day about what was happening at Enron that he was unable or unwilling to share in response to the questions that were being asked. Less than eight months later, on December 2, 2001, Enron would file for bankruptcy protection.

Skilling could see that life as he knew it was unraveling, and he likely could envision a realistic scenario in which he would suffer serious consequences. Attack behavior such as that exhibited by Skilling in that conference call and on the witness stand can be an especially powerful indicator of deception. The more desperate a situation is, the more a person will feel prone to attack. So, when we see this behavior in response to a question, it tells us that the person is particularly highly stressed by that question, and that it's an area that strongly warrants further attention.

One of the deceptive behaviors we introduced in chapter 5 was exhibiting an inappropriate level of concern. As we said, when the facts are not a person's ally, he might resort to a strategy of attempting to diminish the importance of the issue by responding to it in an inappropriately lighthearted manner. In some instances, this behavior could be a form of attack or aggression.

When TV journalist Diane Sawyer conducted her January 28, 2003, interview with Scott Peterson, the Modesto, California, man who was eventually convicted of murdering his pregnant wife, Laci, in one of the highest-profile homicide cases of the decade, she asked him the question everyone wanted her to ask, point-blank: "Did you murder your wife?"

Peterson responded, "No. No. I did not." Oddly, however, he was smiling as he said it. A more inappropriate behavior in response to such a gut-wrenching question is difficult to fathom.

The psychological factors that such behavior might be attributed to are complex, but our experience has shown that a likely element in a reaction like the one exhibited by Peterson is a form of attacking behavior. A smile in response to a question about such a heinous crime might reflect a degree of condescension or dismissiveness that's intended as an assault on the questioner.

Attack behavior can also take the form of a threat, and the threat can even be one that involves self-harm. We saw this during our polygraph days at the Agency, where the stakes were especially high, and the environment in the Polygraph Division was especially tense.

Prior to hooking the subject up to the polygraph machine, there is a pretest interview, which reviews the issues that will be covered during the polygraph examination. This ensures that the subject is confident about his responses, and affords him the opportunity to get anything off his chest that may be directly related to the test question, or to discuss peripheral concerns. At the Agency, these pretest interviews necessarily covered extremely sensitive, personal matters that have to be discussed to determine a person's suitability to be entrusted with information that involves not only our national security, but people's lives. It is an extremely intrusive, invasive procedure that people who have a desire to serve at the Agency subject themselves to.

Susan recalls having to interview one woman four times because of the behaviors she exhibited, and the woman grew increasingly upset. She finally threatened to jump off the Agency's seventh-floor balcony if Susan didn't back off. Those who knew Susan outside of the Agency saw her as a typical soccer mom. This woman branded her the "Bleached Blond Goddess of Torture."

More commonly, the attack behavior in that environment was a direct assault. Because of the particular work she did in the Agency prior to becoming a polygraph examiner, Susan was routinely assigned to polygraph case officers. During the pretest interview of one male case officer, Susan raised the standard question about contact with foreign nationals and foreign intelligence services. That absolutely enraged the case officer—he blew up at Susan, launching into a tirade about how she could never understand the life of a case officer and the activities he or she engages in. Susan was unfazed. She didn't even hook him up to the polygraph machine. Before the end of the pretest interview, the case officer admitted that he had been sleeping with a woman who worked for a foreign intelligence service.

Now, let's delve a little more deeply into how this behavior is typically exhibited in a more extended stimulus-response engagement.

As we noted in chapter 5, Christine O'Donnell, the former U.S. Senate candidate from Delaware, appeared on CNN's *Piers Morgan Tonight* to promote her book. In that chapter we looked at O'Donnell's inconsistent statements. Here, let's focus on her attack behavior.

Well into the interview, Morgan cited a 1996 MTV documentary in which O'Donnell spoke out against masturbation, and he asked her if her views on the matter had changed since then. O'Donnell, who was in a remote studio for the interview, responded that she had addressed the documentary in her book and had explained why she had raised the issue publicly at that point in her life. Morgan referred to other statements O'Donnell had made about abstinence and lust, and used the matter as a segue into a discussion of gay marriage and Don't Ask, Don't Tell. Let's pick up the exchange at that point, and highlight the attack behaviors.

Morgan: It's a natural extension to ask you, for example, a very relevant question for any politician . . .

O'Donnell *(interrupting):* I address it all in the book.

O'Donnell is already squarely in attack mode. The interruption aims to prevent Morgan from getting the question out on the table. This discourteous behavior constitutes an attack on Morgan and the interview strategy and process he is attempting to execute. It strongly suggests that O'Donnell fears Morgan's question will put her in serious harm's way from a political standpoint. As a result, she tries to seize control of the interview and send Morgan a message that she will dictate what is discussed.

Morgan: What is your view of gay marriage, for example?

O'Donnell: I address that stuff in the book. I'm here to talk about . . .

Morgan (*interrupting*): You're on here to promote the damn book, so you can't keep saying, "It's all in the book." You've got to repeat some of it.

O'Donnell: I'm here to talk about the book.

Morgan: Yes, I'm talking about the book. You keep saying, "It's all in the book," so tell me what's in the book.

O'Donnell: Why don't you ask me questions about what I say in the chapter called "Our Follower in Chief," where I criticize Barack Obama? Why don't we talk about . . .

Morgan: Because right now I'm curious about whether you support gay marriage.

O'Donnell: You're borderline being a little bit rude, you know? I obviously . . .

Morgan: Really?

O'Donnell: I obviously want to talk about the issues that I choose to talk about in the book.

At this point in the exchange, O'Donnell has launched a direct attack on Morgan by branding him as "rude." At the same time, her statement that "I'm here to talk about the book" is glaringly inconsistent with her previous responses, in which she refuses to talk about issues that she acknowledges are in the book. In the face of Morgan's persistence on the gay marriage issue, O'Donnell is forced to backtrack and insist on discussing only the issues of her choosing.

Morgan: Do you answer that question in the book?

O'Donnell: I talk about my religious beliefs, yeah, I absolutely do.

Morgan: Do you talk about gay marriage in the book?

O'Donnell: What relevance is that right now? Is there a piece of legislation?

Morgan: It's obviously, as you know, because of Michele Bachmann's views and others', it's obviously a highly contentious political issue. I'm just curious what your view is. You keep saying, "It's in the book." So I'm bemused as to why you wouldn't just say it in an interview, if it's in the book.

O'Donnell: Because I don't think it's relevant. It's not a topic that I choose to embrace, it's not what I'm championing right now. I've been there, done that, gone down that road. Right now what I'm trying to do is to promote a book that I hope to be a very inspirational story to people who are part of the Tea Party movement so that they can continue in this movement to bring America back to the second American Revolution. That's my goal, that's my focus right now.

Here, O'Donnell attacks Morgan by impugning the relevance of his question, and she has again failed to answer it. She clearly fears engaging Morgan on this issue.

Morgan: So would you agree with Michele Bachmann that we should maybe [reinstate] Don't Ask Don't Tell, we should restore that?

O'Donnell: (laughs) I'm not talking about policies. I'm not running for office. Ask Michele Bachmann what she thinks. Ask the candidates who are running for office what they think.

Morgan: Why are you being so weird about this?

O'Donnell: I'm not being weird about this, Piers. I'm not running for office, I'm not promoting a legislative agenda. I'm promoting the policies that I lay out in the book that are mostly fiscal, that are mostly constitutional. That's why I agreed to come on your show, that's what I want to talk about. I'm not being weird, you're being a little rude. *[See chapter 5]*.

Morgan: I'm baffled as to why you think I'm being rude. I think I'm being rather charming and respectful. I'm just asking you questions based on your own public statements, and now what you've written in your own book. It's hardly rude to ask you that, surely.

O'Donnell: Well, don't you think as a host, if I say this is what I want to talk about, that's what we should address?

Morgan: Not really, no. You're a politician.

O'Donnell: Yeah, okay, I'm being pulled away. We turned down another interview for this.

Morgan: Where are you going? You're leaving?

O'Donnell: Well, I was supposed to be speaking at the Republican Women's Club at six o'clock, and I chose to be a little late for that, not to endure a rude talk show host but to talk to you about my book, to talk about the issues I address in my book. Have you read the book?

Morgan: Yes, but these issues are in your book, that's my point. You do talk about them.

O'Donnell: All right. Are we off? Are we done?

O'Donnell ends the interview with a two-pronged attack: dismissing Morgan as a "rude talk show host," and leaving him stranded by abruptly walking off the show.

O'Donnell's behavior in that interview presented a graphic illustration of how a person who feels cornered by a particular line of questioning might be compelled to launch an attack on the questioner as a means of getting him to back off. In this case, O'Donnell appeared to feel threatened by Morgan's questions regarding gay marriage. What should we conclude from the intensity of her attacks in response to that threat? She was likely convinced that engaging Morgan on national TV in a discussion about her views on that topic would hurt her politically, and perhaps would even create problems for her on a more personal level. As O'Donnell saw it, providing truthful information in response to Morgan's questions wasn't an option for her. When the stakes are high and a person feels she has run out of options, aggression often becomes the weapon of choice.

8.

What Deception Looks Like

*He that has eyes to see and ears to hear may convince
himself that no mortal can keep a secret. If his lips are
silent, he chatters with his fingertips; betrayal oozes
out of him at every pore.*

—Sigmund Freud

If a picture is worth a thousand words, this senior corporate executive wrote a book in the course of a single encounter. Phil had been called in to interview the executive, who worked for a Fortune 500 company that had a government contract. Due to the classified nature of the work to be performed under the contract, background investigations had been conducted on a number of the executives in the company, including this one—we'll call him "Norman." Norman's background check had revealed that he had a foreign girlfriend. Although he was married, the issue wasn't so much that Norman had a girlfriend, but that he had not disclosed it. He was required to make all foreign-national contacts a matter of record, and he had failed to do so.

Norman was a formidable presence, a big guy who had played football in college. His demeanor was brusque when he came in, hung up his suit coat, and sat down. Phil explained to him why he was there: to talk to him about the report that he had a foreign girlfriend. In response to that, Norman said, "Okay," and he took off his right shoe, pulled his foot up into his chair, and wrapped his arms around his knee. Then, when Phil asked him directly whether he had a foreign girlfriend, Norman responded with a couple of convincing statements, took off his left shoe, tucked his left foot into the chair, and wrapped his arms around both knees. So there was Norman, this big man in a crisp white shirt and tie, sitting in a fetal position, peering between his legs at Phil.

What was Phil to make of this? Clearly, Norman had to have a certain level of intellect and sophistication to have become a senior executive at a Fortune 500 company, yet he had absolutely no awareness of the behavior he was exhibiting. It was a glaring illustration of how no one is immune from exhibiting assessable behavior. Let's just say Phil knew he had a problem, and that he had more work to do.

We said in chapter 2 that the majority of communication is nonverbal. In fact, nonverbals comprise a fairly significant majority. The findings vary in different studies, but most researchers have concluded that at least two-thirds of our communication is accomplished nonverbally. If we consider that category of communication in its entirety and think of it as "body language," it's important to understand that the deceptive nonverbal behaviors we examine as part of the model are only a subset of that. In other words, some forms of body language are considerably more revealing than others.

So-called body language "experts" tend to analyze nonverbal behaviors globally. Remember what we said about global behavior assessment? You don't want to go there, because you'd be trying to get that drink from the fire hose, and you'd be putting yourself in the position of having to guess at the meaning and significance of a particular posture or repetitive motion. You need to take the guesswork out of the equation, and filter out all of those global behaviors that do nothing to help you get to where you want to go: identifying deception. So, you need to limit your analysis to only those behaviors that come in direct, timely response to the stimulus, which is your question.

Experience has enabled us to identify certain behaviors as potentially being deceptive when exhibited in this manner. Let's examine them.

BEHAVIORAL PAUSE OR DELAY. You ask a person a question and you initially get nothing. After a delay, he begins to respond. How long does a delay have to be before it's meaningful, before you would consider it a deceptive indicator? Well, it depends.

Try this exercise on a friend: Ask her the question, "On

this date seven years ago, what were you doing that day?" The person will invariably pause before responding, because it's not a question that naturally evokes an immediately response—the person has to think about it, and likely still won't be able to offer a meaningful response. Now ask her, "On this date seven years ago, did you rob a gas station?" If your friend pauses before responding, you probably need to choose your friends more carefully. Much more likely, there will be no pause—your friend will immediately respond, "No!" or "Of course not!" It's a simple exercise, but it drives home the point that the delay needs to be considered in the context of whether it's appropriate for the question.

A second variable is whether the delay is appropriate for the person. In the course of an interview, for example, a pattern will naturally develop that gives you a sense of how much time elapses before the person responds to your questions. If we see something that falls outside of that established pattern, then we have a concern.

VERBAL/NONVERBAL DISCONNECT. Our brains are wired in a way that causes our verbal and nonverbal behaviors to naturally match up. So when there's a disconnect, we consider that a potential deceptive indicator.

A common verbal/nonverbal disconnect to watch out for occurs when a person nods affirmatively while saying, "No," or turns his head from side to side while saying, "Yes." As an exercise, if you were to perform that mismatch in response to a question, you'd find that you really have to force yourself through the motion. Yet, a deceptive person will potentially do it without even thinking about it.

There are a couple of caveats associated with this particular indicator. First, this indicator is only applicable in a narrative response, not in a one-word or short-phrase response. Consider, for example, that a person's head might make a sharp nodding motion when he says "No!" That's not a disconnect; it's simple emphasis. Second, it's important to keep in mind that in some cultures, a nodding motion doesn't mean "yes," and a side-to-side head motion doesn't mean "no." So, you need to ensure you're familiar with the cultural patterns of the person who's being questioned.

HIDING THE MOUTH OR EYES. A deceptive person will often hide her mouth or eyes when she's being untruthful. There is a natural tendency to want to cover over a lie, so if a person's hand goes in front of her mouth while she's responding to a question, that's significant. Similarly, there's a natural inclination to shield oneself from the reaction of those who are being lied to. If a person shields her eyes while she's responding to a question, what she might well be indicating, on a subconscious level, is that she can't bear to see the reaction to the whopper she's telling. This shielding may be accomplished with a hand, or the person might even close her eyes. We're not referring to blinking here, but if a person closes her eyes while responding to a question that does not require reflection to answer, we consider that a means of hiding the eyes, and a likely deceptive indicator.

THROAT-CLEARING OR SWALLOWING. If a person clears his throat or performs a significant swallow prior to answering the question, that's a potential problem. If he does it after he answers, that doesn't bother us. But if he does it before he answers, a couple of things might be happening. He might be doing the nonverbal equivalent of the verbal "I swear to God . . ."—dressing up the lie in its Sunday best before presenting it to us. Or physiologically, the question might have created a spike in anxiety, which can cause discomfort or dryness in the mouth and throat.

HAND-TO-FACE ACTIVITY. While you're in L-squared mode, be on the lookout for anything a person does with his face or in the head region in response to your question. This often takes the form of biting or licking the lips, or pulling on the lips or ears. The reason goes back to simple high school science. You've asked a question, and the question creates a spike in anxiety because a truthful response would be incriminating. That, in turn, triggers the autonomic nervous system to go to work to dissipate the anxiety. One of the ways it does that is by kicking in the fight-or-flight response. The person's body is rerouting circulation to his vital organs and major muscle groups so he can run faster, jump higher, fight harder in response to the threat. Where does that blood come from? It comes from blood-rich regions of the body that can temporarily do with a diminished supply of blood—typically, the surfaces of the face, the ears, and the extremities. When the blood rushes away from those regions, it irritates the capillaries, which can create a sensation of cold or itchiness. Without the person even realizing it, his hands are drawn to those areas, or there's a wringing or rubbing of the hands. *Boom!*—you've spotted a deceptive indicator.

ANCHOR-POINT MOVEMENT. Beyond these physiological reactions, the body also dissipates this anxiety through other forms of physical activity, most notably "anchor-point" movements.

A person's anchor points are those parts of his body that anchor him in a particular spot or position. If a person is standing, his primary anchor points are his feet. His secondary anchor points might be his arms if they're folded in front of him, or they might be his hands if he's standing with his hands on his hips or in his pockets. We're not worried about his posture; we're only looking at those anchor points.

If a person is sitting in a chair, his primary anchor points would be his buttocks, his back, and his feet. We always consider both feet as anchor points, even if he has his legs crossed and one foot is in the air. In fact, if everything else is locked down, that foot in the air might be the most likely anchor point to move as the body works to dissipate anxiety, because it's the point of least resistance. Secondary anchor points might be an elbow on the arm of the chair, or hands resting in the lap. Bear in mind that we do not consider each anchor-point movement as a separate deceptive indicator. So, if there is anchor point movement in response to your question, regardless of how many anchor points move, count that as just one deceptive behavior.

It's worth mentioning here that when we interview someone, the last place we would want the interviewee to sit is in a straight-back chair with four legs. We want the person in a chair that has wheels, that rocks and swivels, that might even have moveable arm rests. That type of chair becomes a behavioral amplifier, magnifying those anchor-point movements and making them particularly easy to spot.

GROOMING GESTURES. Another way that some people may dissipate anxiety is through physical activity in the form of grooming oneself or the immediate surroundings. Let's get a sense of what this looks like.

Our colleague Don Tennant tells the story of having interviewed the CEO of a major U.S. software company when he was working as a technology journalist in Hong Kong. The early-morning interview was conducted in the presidential suite of the Grand Hyatt Hong Kong, where the CEO was staying. When Don arrived, the CEO answered the door in a Hugh-Hefner-esque bathrobe, and welcomed him to have a seat in the living room near the grand piano.

At this particular time in the company's history, the CEO

was on the verge of introducing a hardware device to the market, a gutsy move that had created a huge buzz in the tech sector, but that some analysts considered to be horribly ill-advised. There appeared to be no real synergy between the company's massive software business and an effort to market a hardware device, but the CEO was adamant that taking that risk would prove to be one of the best decisions he ever made.

Given the controversy surrounding the new strategy, Don circled back to the topic of the hardware device several times during the course of the hour-long interview, and each time the CEO insisted that the hardware product would be hugely successful and would deliver tremendous shareholder value. What was fascinating, however, was that each time he proclaimed that the device would be a success, the CEO would grasp the belt of his bathrobe and cinch the robe tighter. As Don has pointed out on any number of occasions since then, he had no problem with that, because he didn't know what the CEO had on under there. But the consistency of the grooming gesture was striking.

As it turned out, the hardware device was a colossal failure, and the idea was eventually shelved. The company hasn't ventured into the hardware realm since.

In a more typical setting, when responding to a question, a deceptive man might adjust his tie or shirt cuffs, or maybe his glasses. An untruthful woman might move a few strands of hair behind her ear, or straighten her skirt. We're also concerned with sweat management. That a person might be sweating doesn't bother us, but if he takes out his handker-chief (or, perhaps more likely, a hand sans kerchief) and wipes the sweat off his brow when responding to a question, that's significant.

Tidying up the surroundings is another form of grooming gesture. You ask a question, and suddenly the phone isn't turned the right way, the glass of water is too close, or the pencil isn't in the right place. Like anchor-point movements, count all of these grooming gestures that come within the response to a single question as a single deceptive indicator.

9 ·

Truth in the Lie: Spying Unintended Messages

*I apologize for lying to you. I promise I won't deceive
you except in matters of this sort.*

— *Spiro T. Agnew*

On April 29, 2001, *The New York Times* published a story by
Alex Berenson about Computer Associates, a giant main-
frame software company headquartered on Long Island that
had a reputation for being ruthless with its competitors, and
nearly as hard-nosed with its employees and customers. The
story, headlined "A Software Company Runs Out of Tricks;
The Past May Haunt Computer Associates," exposed what, according to former employees, was a long-standing, systematic
plan to overstate its revenue and profits. The company inflated
its reported income, the former employees said, by means of
an accounting procedure that made new product sales appear
to be more robust than they really were. In short, Computer

Associates was alleged to have engaged in widespread accounting fraud.

The charges were so damning that Computer Associates's CEO, Sanjay Kumar, was compelled to appear on CNBC the same day to refute them. In an interview with CNBC's Bill Griffeth, Kumar started off by attacking the *Times* for publishing the article without naming the sources or quoting any Wall Street analysts. Then Griffeth asked him about the charge that the company was attempting to mask a decline in sales. Within Kumar's response was this nugget: "And our new business model, by the way, is two things: It's a new way of selling and a new way of counting revenue."

Later in the interview, Griffeth asked Kumar about an issue raised in the *Times* article about confusing software maintenance revenue with new software business revenue. Kumar responded by stressing the strictness of GAAP accounting rules, and then he said this:

> And we also, by the way, further detailed in our call this morning and there's information on our Web site as to why our maintenance numbers are in the range, but at the low end of the range, of software companies. And that's a perfectly plausible answer. We don't need to have maintenance numbers like anybody else, but we're not doing anything wrong, fundamentally, in our business.

Now, fast-forward to November 2, 2006. On that day, Kumar was sentenced to twelve years in prison for his role in perpetrating $2.2 billion in accounting fraud at Computer Associates, after pleading guilty to charges of securities fraud and obstruction of justice. Today, he is prisoner No. 71321-053 at the Federal Correctional Institution Satellite Camp in Fairton, New Jersey.

That the sentencing day would eventually come was practically foretold in that 2001 CNBC interview. We've analyzed the full transcript of the interview, and we found that Kumar exhibited more than thirty deceptive behaviors. For our purpose here, we want to focus on the excerpts we cited above, because they're rather stunning illustrations of what we call "unintended messages," or, more colorfully, "truth in the lie."

If a deceptive person finds himself in a hole because he's been asked a question about a matter in which the facts are not his ally, he's obviously not in a position to respond with the facts. In the process of developing a response, then, he makes a conscious decision to take a particular tack. Perhaps he'll concentrate on convincing the questioner of his morality; maybe he'll go the evasive route and try to deflect the question; or he might feel compelled to go into attack mode as a means of getting the questioner to back off. What he's not aware of, however, is that often in that process, without even realizing it, he'll say things that reveal what in reality he knows to be the truth.

When Kumar said that Computer Associates's new business model was "a new way of selling and a new way of counting revenue," he unintentionally conveyed an incriminating
message about the company's accounting procedures. After
all, what is accounting fraud if not "a new way of counting
revenue?" Similarly, when he said his response to the maintenance revenue question was a perfectly "plausible" answer,
you only need to consider the definition of "plausible"—
superficially reasonable or believable, or having the appearance of the truth—to get the unintended message that Kumar's
aim was to convey something that was believable, since he
wasn't in a position to convey the truth. And then, to top it
off, he stressed that Computer Associates was doing nothing
"fundamentally" wrong in its business. What he didn't realize
he told the world is that there was, on some level, *something*
wrong with the way it was doing business.

In each of these cases, Kumar was making a concerted effort to cover up the truth. But what he ended up communicat-
ing was that there were other things he could say in order to
be truthful, and that he wasn't going to reveal them.

Ten years later, in the autumn of 2011, another businessman
was having problems with the media. This time the businessman was Herman Cain, the former restaurateur who had
entered the race to become the Republican nominee for

president of the United States. Just when it appeared Cain had managed to escape the fallout from allegations made by two women that he had subjected them to sexual harassment in the 1990s, a bombshell dropped. In its evening newscast on November 28, an Atlanta TV station aired an interview with Ginger White, an Atlanta businesswoman who claimed that she and Cain had engaged in an on-again, off-again affair for more than thirteen years.

The TV station had informed Cain earlier in the day that it was planning to air the interview that evening, so Cain decided to try to get in front of the story by appearing on CNN's *The Situation Room with Wolf Blitzer* a couple of hours before the TV station's newscast to deny the allegation. In his interview with Blitzer, Cain admitted that he had known White for those thirteen years, but insisted that it was just a friendship, and that he had provided some financial assistance to her simply because she was a friend in need.

Cain exited the presidential race on December 3, just five days after his interview with Blitzer. He continues to maintain that all of the allegations are false, as he did throughout the interview with Blitzer. Cain insisted that White's allegation would be shown to be baseless, as he claimed the sexual harassment allegations had been. It is indeed the case that when this book went to publication, none of the allegations were proven to be true, so our analysis of the interview is simply a behavioral assessment based on our application of the model. Here, then, is an excerpt from the transcript of that interview:

> **Blitzer:** What did [the Atlanta TV station] say to you?
>
> **Cain:** They just said, you know, they mentioned the name of the individual . . .
>
> **Blitzer:** And you know this woman?
>
> **Cain:** And I do know who she is, and they mentioned what the accusation is going to be. But until the story comes out, I'm not at liberty to respond to something at this point. Now, when the story breaks, through my attorney, Lin Wood of Atlanta, Georgia, we will respond. We chased all of these other rumors for two weeks before, and as it turned out, they were baseless. Why? Because they weren't able to come up with any documentation, any proof, or anything that was credible. And so we will address these when they come out. But at this point I just wanted to give you a heads-up. I don't have anything to hide, and we will address every one of the details as we know them.

Later in the interview, Cain reiterated his contention that the sexual harassment allegations were baseless:

Blitzer: But this . . . As you understand, the two women who have accused you of sexual harassment, now a third woman potentially coming out and saying she had an affair with you . . .

Cain: And remember that the first two were baseless—they were false accusations. They were not able to prove it and I went before the media and public and said here's what I know, here are the facts, and people will have to make that judgment as to whether or not they believe me or believe them. The same is true of the one that is supposed to be reported on later today.

Now, let's examine the key statements: "*We chased all of these other rumors for two weeks before, and as it turned out, they were baseless. Why? Because they weren't able to come up with any documentation, any proof, or anything that was credible.*" And further: "*And remember that the first two were baseless—they were false accusations. They were not able to prove it.*"

Applying the model, we see an unintended message in Cain's statement: The sexual harassment allegations were "baseless" and "false" not because Cain didn't commit the sexual harassment, but because his accusers couldn't prove it. It's interesting that it was in that context that Cain added, "The same is true of the one that is supposed to be reported on later today."

In fact, elsewhere in the interview, Cain conveyed another unintended message in reference to the question of whether he and White had had sex. Here's the excerpt:

Blitzer: And when you say "friend"—these are awkward questions, but I'll ask you the questions you're going to be asked—was this an affair?

Cain: No, it was not.

Blitzer: There was no sex?

Cain: No.

Blitzer: None?

Cain: No.

Blitzer: And if this woman says there is, she's lying? Is that what you're . . .

Cain: Well, Wolf, let's see what the story's going to be. I don't want to get into being pinned down on some things until we see what the story's going to be.

When Cain said he didn't want to "get into being pinned down on some things until we see what the story's going to be," that was a true statement. But, based on the model, the unintended message was clear: If White says there was sex, he can't say she's lying.

So how can you train yourself to spot this truth in the lie, or unintended messaging? Understand that when you're dealing with a situation in which truth matters, literalness becomes very important. Remember in chapter 2, when we said that one of the problems with communication is that when we hear something, we put our own spin on it, and that's what we use to define the actions we take? When you're speaking with someone with the aim of obtaining truthful information, it's critically important to capture exactly what the person says, and to consider what's literally being communicated to you.

Several years ago, we were contacted by the head of investigations for a large, family-owned corporation. The security head, an ex-FBI agent we'll call "Steve," said the company had received a call from a man who claimed he had been approached by some thugs to help them in a plot to kidnap the family's children.

The call was traced to a man in South America—let's call him "Raul"—and it was transferred to Steve, who over the course of a lengthy phone conversation with Raul asked all the right questions to collect valuable information about the threat. Raul said he was willing to provide more details as the planning progressed, and near the end of the call requested two hundred dollars as an advance for overnight shipping charges to send video evidence on the plot discussions. It was initially treated as a serious, viable threat, and there was no information available to refute it.

Steve brought us into the investigation to get our assessment of the legitimacy of the threat. We examined the transcripts of the phone conversation between Steve and Raul, and we found one exchange particularly interesting. Steve was relentless in pressing Raul for information on the plot and what the thugs had asked him to do. Raul seemed agitated, but he provided more details.

"Is that it?" Steve asked.

"Hey, look," Raul replied. "I've told you more than they told me."

That was the spy-the-lie moment. After all, how could that be? The unintended message Raul conveyed with that statement was, "I'm making this up as I go along."

Steve had done an outstanding job of getting the information we needed to conduct our analysis. We identified a number of deceptive behaviors and unintended messages, and we were able to conclude that the threat was bogus. Further investigation revealed that Raul had made the same extortion attempt against other high-net-worth families in the past, and he was arrested as a result of the investigation. Today, Raul is in prison.

Certainly, unintended messages are just as commonly conveyed in everyday situations that are far removed from criminal wrongdoing. Phil recalls doing a preemployment screening interview for a client who was concerned about whether the candidate would be truly loyal and committed to establishing herself with the company. The last thing the client wanted was a job-hopper. At one point in the interview, Phil asked the candidate what she would say to convince her prospective employer that she was the right person for the job.

"I would tell him that I'm well qualified and I have the skills he's looking for," she replied. "And he'll miss me when I'm gone."

That unintended message was all Phil and the client needed to hear.

Now, let's delve into unintended messages a little more deeply. A particular question that often causes revealing unintended messages to surface is one we call the "Punishment Question." You ask the suspect, "What do you think should happen to the person who did this?"

This question has been routinely asked in interviews of suspects since at least the 1970s, and it's probably the least understood and most misused question employed by law enforcement officers today. If you are interviewing the guilty party, you are, in effect, asking the person to sentence himself. The theory is that the guilty party will, naturally, suggest a relatively light punishment. On the other hand, the theory goes, the response of a person who is innocent will likely reflect a stiffer punishment, and an especially harsh one for heinous crimes.

The problem with this theory is that it's easy for some to see through the thrust of the question, so deceptive people respond with what they presume we expect to hear from a truthful, innocent person. Not uncommonly, they respond with a harsh punishment—something like "He should be locked up for life."

Remember, deceptive people are always looking for ways to manage our perception, which is one of the reasons it's so vitally important to ignore truthful behavior. We've worked with dozens of law enforcement agencies in a consulting or training capacity, and it's remarkable how frequently we see seasoned detectives and other investigators make mistakes stemming from an erroneous analysis of responses to this question.

Analyzing a response to the Punishment Question requires caution. We are completely unfazed by a response that advocates strong punishment, because it's a response that's equally likely to come from truthful and deceptive people. On the other hand, our experience has demonstrated that if a suspect's response reflects an abnormally lenient punishment, that raises a red flag that suggests we're dealing with a deceptive person. Let's examine what this looks like in actual cases.

Michael once interviewed a twenty-year-old male who eventually confessed to having sexual contact with two females, ages twelve and thirteen. Here's an excerpt from the transcript of that interview:

Michael: If somebody did what they say you did, what do you think should happen to somebody who did that, if it was up to you?

Suspect: I have to think about this. You mean the allegations I'm accused of, right? Um, I mean, I would not want jail time. I think anybody who goes into jail is going to come out with a whole other mind. Um, should be . . . should be, you know, taking some kind of course or something. Maybe they have problems. A psych . . . I don't know . . . counseling? Maybe an apology, definitely, if that's what they wanted. I don't know, um, or if it was something they, the family, requested and the person had to do.

An apology seems fairly lenient, wouldn't you say? But getting back to those unintended messages, consider that statement, *"I would not want jail time."* He thinks he's telling Michael that he would not want whoever did it to have jail time. But by focusing on literalness, we get the unintended message: "I did it, but I don't want to go to jail."

Then there was the case of a convicted felon who was driving in rural Nevada, and ran out of gas miles from the nearest gas station. There was a ranch a short distance away where a pickup truck was parked, and the suspect took it and drove to the gas station to get a can of gas. The owner of the

A TIP FOR PARENTS

When you were a kid and your parents found out about something you did that you shouldn't have done (not that it isn't next to impossible to think of any such circumstance, of course), did they ever ask you what you thought your punishment should be? It was probably their way of getting you to really think about what you had done and the consequences of your actions. Perhaps they were also trying to give you some sense of the unappealing position you had put them in by forcing them to dole out punishment.

If you've since become a parent yourself, perhaps you've posed the same question to a child whose behavior warranted some sort of discipline. But what about a situation in which you're not certain whether your child was at fault? Could the same question help you to determine your child's culpability?

Let's say you come home from work and there's a grape-juice stain on the couch. You have two

pickup saw him take the truck, and called the police. The suspect was apprehended at gunpoint by the state Highway Patrol at the gas station.

When Michael interviewed him, he initially claimed that he had gotten permission from the truck's owner, and had given him some money for loaning the truck to him. The suspect desperately needed the authorities to buy that story. His criminal record included rape, kidnapping, grand theft auto, receiving stolen property, robbery, and various drug and alcohol arrests, and he had spent most of his life in prison. Because of his record, he was looking at twenty-five years to life for taking the pickup truck. This is how the Punishment Question went down:

Michael: What do you think should happen to someone who would take someone else's truck without permission?

Suspect: It depends on the criminal history of the person.

Michael: Let's say someone with your criminal history.

Suspect: Well, he definitely doesn't deserve life, but he deserves punishment. A punishment, it's hard to call. It depends on the inside of the person, what's going on, the character. I truthfully can't answer that.

The unintended messaging was clear: With his statement that *"he definitely doesn't deserve life, but he deserves punishment,"* the suspect was negotiating his own sentence. When he said, *"I truthfully can't answer that,"* what he was telling Michael, without realizing it, was that he couldn't bring himself to answer the question truthfully because he would be sentencing himself. He later confessed to taking the truck without permission.

children, both of whom like grape juice, and both of whom know full well that they're not allowed to eat or drink on the couch. You ask both of them if they know how the grape-juice stain got there, and they both insist they have no idea.

Try speaking with them individually, and ask them both what they think the punishment should be for whomever had been drinking grape juice on the couch. As always, follow the cluster rule. But also consider the leniency of the suggested punishment. If Tommy says, "No computer for a week," and Tammy says, "No grape juice for a week," you probably have more work to do with Tammy. Also, be aware that the culprit will sometimes avoid answering the punishment question altogether. Tammy might not say anything at all, or she might muster that barely audible "I don't know."

Another case involved a twenty-five-year-old father who was accused of injuring his three-month-old son. Michael interviewed the mother first, and determined that she had nothing to do with the baby's injuries, which included broken ribs, a swollen liver, and bruises on his back. He then interviewed the father, who initially denied inflicting the injuries. Deceptive behaviors included anchor-point movements and a verbal/nonverbal disconnect—he nodded affirmatively as he stated his denial. And then came the Punishment Question:

Michael: What do you think should happen to the person who did this?

Father *(after repeating the question)***:** It's really a touchy thing. They definitely need to get some help. They definitely need to be evaluated. I definitely think they should get some serious, serious help.

Aside from the abnormal leniency—it was hardly a response that a father of a seriously injured baby would offer if someone else had inflicted the injuries—we once again have truth in the lie: *"It's really a touchy thing."* The unintended message conveyed to Michael was, "That question is really sensitive and it makes me really uncomfortable because I'm the one who did it." The father ultimately confessed. As is the case in so many of these tragedies, the motive was "frustration."

10.

You Don't Ask, You Don't Get

*All truths are easy to understand once they are
discovered; the point is to discover them.*

—*Galileo Galilei*

At 1:35 on the afternoon of Monday, June 13, 1994, Los Angeles Police Department detective Phil Vannatter switched on the tape recorder. He and his partner, Detective Tom Lange, were in an interview room in Parker Center, the LAPD headquarters, with a man in his late forties who appeared tired and haggard. Vannatter and Lange had been assigned to investigate a double homicide that had taken place the night before—brutal stabbings that took the lives of Nicole Brown Simpson and her friend, Ron Goldman. The haggard interview subject was O. J. Simpson, the sports hero turned movie star whose marriage to Nicole had ended two years earlier. Vannatter began the interview by reading Simpson his

Miranda rights, and Simpson agreed to speak with the detectives without having his attorney present.

Let's pause right there. Let's imagine that you had been assigned to the case, and that you're the one who is interviewing Simpson. You have an advantage that Vannatter and Lange, through no fault of their own, didn't have—one that could prove to be an invaluable asset: You have the model. You have Simpson sitting in a swiveling desk chair that will amplify his nonverbal behaviors, and there is nothing blocking your view of his body. But as you switch on the recorder and settle into your seat, you recognize a cold, hard fact: The model is only as good as the questions you ask in the course of employing it.

You know it's essential that you ask the right questions, and you're aware that this particular interview is especially critical. It's not just that Simpson is the ex-husband, and that there had been reports of domestic violence during the marriage. You had declared Simpson's home a crime scene that morning, and obtained a search warrant, after finding an apparent blood stain on his Ford Bronco. And Simpson has a suspicious bandaged cut on his hand.

So as you begin the interview, the most important piece of information you want to know is obvious: Did Simpson commit the murders? But if you were to go straight for the jugular and ask him that question, you might have a problem. If O.J. did it, he knows he's going to be asked that question in one form or another. If he's made the decision to lie about it, he only has to get one word out of his mouth to accomplish his goal: "No." He has the advantage.

To prevent that, your approach needs to focus on questions that Simpson is less likely to be prepared for, and more likely to compel him to provide information you want—or, failing that, to exhibit behavior that you can read. Take your detective hat off for a moment, and consider what your mind-set would be if you were a guilty Simpson. You find yourself in a nightmarish situation: You did something unspeakably horrific last night, and you're

Simpson: We were leaving a dance recital. She took off and I was talking to her parents.

Vannatter: Where was the dance recital?

Simpson: Paul Revere High School.

Vannatter: And was that for one of your children?

Simpson: For my daughter Sydney.

Vannatter: And what time was that yesterday?

Simpson: It ended about six-thirty, quarter to seven, something like that, you know in the ballpark, right in that area. And they took off.

Vannatter: They?

Simpson: Her and her family, her

mother and father, sisters, my kids, you know.

As you can see, if Simpson was guilty, he never lost the advantage. He was able to stick to the script he had likely prepared in his mind to respond to the question about when he had last seen Nicole, a question he was almost certainly expecting. For the next fourteen minutes, Simpson remained in the driver's seat, responding comfortably to questions about the cars he drove, his girlfriend Paula Barbieri, his overnight trip to Chicago for a golf tournament, the cut on his hand, more about his relationship with Nicole, what he was wearing the previous night, and his hectic schedule. At just over 18 minutes into the interview,

not even sure why you did it. You just lost control, went crazy for a few surreal moments, and now you're scared to death. Your only strategy at this point is to try to figure out how this whole investigative and legal process is going to unfold, and you're simply trying to stay one step ahead of the game. You've found yourself having been summoned to the LAPD headquarters to be interviewed, and you know you're a reasonable suspect because of some issues that you and Nicole have had over the years. You know they're going to ask you if you did it, and you know you're going to say, "No." So you show up at Parker Center, and the detectives take you to an interview room and read you your Miranda rights. Now, imagine that the interview begins something like the following:

"O.J., first of all, thank you very much for coming in. We appreciate your willingness to do that. We know you're very concerned about your children, and that you're eager to get back to them to ensure they're okay. So while there is a lot that we'd like to cover, we're going to stick

YOU DON'T ASK, YOU DON'T GET

to the most important issues. O.J., I think the most important thing we need to ask you about is, what happened at Nicole's last night?"

Silence. You have to process the question. What it is that's causing you to have to process it, aside from the fact that you didn't expect it, rests in the type of question you're dealing with. "What happened at Nicole's last night?" is a *presumptive question*, one that presumes something about the matter at hand. In this case, "What happened at Nicole's last night?" presumes that there is a possibility that Simpson was at Nicole's home, and that he has some information that he hasn't shared.

It's important to distinguish a presumptive question from a *leading question*. A leading question is one that puts words in the person's mouth and directs him to an answer: "You were at Nicole's last night, weren't you?"

To understand why presumptive questions are so powerful, take your "guilty Simpson" hat off, and put your "innocent Simpson" hat on. If you were innocent

Vannatter abruptly changed the subject from Simpson's hectic schedule:

Vannatter: O.J., we've got sort of a problem.

Simpson: Mmm-hmm.

Vannatter: We've got some blood on and in your car, we've got some blood at your house, and it's sort of a problem.

Simpson: Well, take my blood—test it.

Lange: Well, we'd like to do that. We've got, of course, the cut on your finger that you aren't real clear on. Do you recall having that cut on your finger the last time you were at Nicole's house?

Simpson: [pause] A week ago?

Lange: Yeah.

Simpson: No, it was last night.

Lange: Okay, so it was last night you cut it?

Vannatter: Somewhere after the recital?

Simpson: Somewhere when I was rushing to get out of my house.

Vannatter: Okay, after the recital?

Simpson: Yeah.

Vannatter: What do you think happened? Do you have any idea?

Simpson: I have no idea, man. You guys haven't told me anything. I have no idea what happened. When you said, too, my daughter had said something to me

and you were asked precisely the same question, you would immediately know the answer—you wouldn't have to hesitate. You might say something like "All I know is that she was killed."

But with your "guilty Simpson" hat on, you have to process that. Now you have to factor in what the detectives might know, and determine how that will impact your game plan.

That's going to take some time, so you're likely to pause, and attempt to buy yourself some time to formulate your response:

"What happened at Nicole's last night? You're asking me what happened? How would I know what happened? I wasn't anywhere near there last night!"

Time to put your detective hat back on. At that point, Simpson is likely feeling that his game plan is intact. So what would your next question be? You might instinctively be inclined to ask, "Where were you last night?" But there's a potential problem with that, and it's the same problem that arose with the "Did you do it?" question: Simpson is almost certainly anticipating it, and has a response prepared for it. By giving him the opportunity to get that response out on the table, you've allowed him to stick to his strategy, which makes your job more difficult. Suppose, instead, that after Simpson gave you a deceptive response to your question about what happened at Nicole's last night, your next question went something like this:

"Okay, O.J., I understand. Let me explain to you that obviously, this is a very important case because of who you are. I know you would want us to have every available officer working on this case, and I can assure you we do—every resource we can muster is being tapped to resolve it. As a matter of fact, as we speak, we have officers scouring Nicole's neighborhood, trying to figure this out. O.J., is there any reason that any of the neighbors will tell us that they saw you in the neighborhood last night?"

Again, silence. You've asked a question that, like the previous one, put Simpson in processing mode. This time, your question is what we call a *bait question*. A

today that somebody else might have been involved. I have absolutely no idea what happened. I don't know how, why, or what. I mean, you guys haven't told me anything. Every time I ask you guys, you say you're going to tell me in a bit.

Vannatter: Well, we don't know a lot of the answers to these questions yet ourselves, O.J., okay?

Instead of beginning the interview with the presumptive question, "O.J., what happened at Nicole's last night?" the detectives gave Simpson eighteen minutes to entrench himself in his story, and then asked that key question in the form of an opinion question: "What do you think happened? Do you have any idea?" Simpson

*was off the hook—
the way Vannatter
phrased the question,
the presumption was
that Simpson wasn't
at Nicole's the night
before, and that he
was therefore left to
speculate on what
happened. That made
it extraordinarily easy
for Simpson to say, "I
have no idea." After
that, the detectives
were at even more of
a disadvantage. The
final twelve minutes
of the interview deliv-
ered little of any
substance.
Might the right ques-
tions have ultimately
yielded a confession
on that very first day
of the investigation?
We'll never know. But
we do know what
happens when the
wrong questions are
asked.*

bait question is a hypothetical question that operates on a psychological principle called a "mind virus." You've probably experienced how a mind virus works.

Imagine that you walk into work on Monday morning, and a coworker comes up to you and says, "The boss wants to see you in her office right away." You ask what she wants, and your coworker says, "I don't know, but she said 'right away.'" Is your likely reaction one of excitement because you're thinking today's the day you're going to get that long-awaited raise? Probably not. You're more likely to start thinking about whether something is wrong, and if so, what the problem might be. The virus begins to spread. Your mind is racing as you come up with various scenarios, trying to determine what the likely issues are, and how you should respond to each issue. You begin to consider the consequences of each situation. And before you know it, the virus has enveloped you.

People often make decisions on the basis of this viral thinking, and baits take advantage of that fact by posing a hypothetical question. A very effective phrase to use is, "Is there any reason . . . ?" Bear in mind that the more implicit your language, the stronger the mind virus—when you become more explicit, the person has more of a chance to evaluate it. If you were to ask Simpson if there's any reason the next-door neighbor will say he saw him there, you're giving him a better chance of overcoming it. He might happen to know the next-door neighbor is out of town, so he immediately responds, "No." Broader, then, is better.

Now, it's important to distinguish between a bait and a *bluff*. Contrary to what we often see from Hollywood, bluffs very rarely work.

Suppose that with your detective hat on, you say to Simpson, "We have somebody who says he saw you in Nicole's neighborhood last night." O.J. may know or strongly suspect that you're bluffing, so he responds accordingly, and asks, "Who?" And the moment you show reluctance or refuse to share that information with him, you become the enemy. Instead of getting cooperation, you now have likely widened

PRESENT A CLEAR STIMULUS

Remember, the model is only as good as the questions you ask in the course of employing it. Since the behavior you're analyzing is the direct result of a stimulus—your question—it follows that your presentation of the stimulus is critical to the accuracy and usefulness of your analysis. Here are four tips to keep in mind when you formulate your question to ensure that it's as clear as you can make it:

Keep it short. When possible, keep your question shorter rather than longer. As we noted in chapter 3, the individual you're questioning is likely thinking ten times faster than you're speaking. So if you ask a long, drawn-out, rambling question, that can be problematic if his agenda is to try to avoid answering your question or to provide a response that's misleading.

Keep it simple. Some people try to convey their level of intellect by means of complex sentence structure and highbrow vocabulary. Make sure you don't fall into that trap—if the person doesn't fully understand your question, his response is less likely to be behaviorally significant. Beyond that, you might see behavior that appears deceptive, when the stimulus of that behavior is nothing more than his confusion.

Keep it singular in meaning. If your question is ambiguous, you have

the gap between your interests and his interests. When you stick with a bait, you're on solid ground.

If Simpson is guilty, what might his response be to the question, "Is there any reason that any of the neighbors will tell us that they saw you there last night?" He may feel it's in his best interest to allow for that possibility, so he might say something like "I do occasionally pass through the neighborhood and sometimes I stop to check on the kids, and now that I think about it I did drive through last night, but I didn't see any lights on, so I didn't stop." If he does give you an answer like that, you've asked two questions and already you're fairly confident he's not being truthful—you've even placed him in the vicinity of the crime. You don't have full advantage yet, because he hasn't confessed. But you're making progress.

A beautiful thing about presumptive and bait questions is that they aren't in any way contrary to the facts of the situation. They're fair, because the truthful person can respond without processing them. If Simpson wasn't there, all he has to do is say, "No."

Presumptive and bait questions have a couple of things in common, aside from being extremely powerful. First, they both have a limited shelf life in the information collection process. If you overuse them, the person is likely going to figure out what you're doing. It will trigger his defenses, and he'll view you as an adversary who's trying to trick or mislead him in some way. We've found that generally, presumptive and bait questions should each be used no more than two or three times in the course of an hour-long interaction.

Second, while all questions should be delivered as neutrally as possible, neutrality is especially important with presumptive and bait questions—the person needs to feel that you have no preconceived notions about how he's going to answer each question. This neutrality is conveyed by the words you use to frame the question, and the tone or demeanor you use to deliver it. It needs to be delivered in a very matter-of-fact manner, with no additional

no way of knowing how the person understood the question. If you observe a deceptive behavior, you don't know what he's reacting to. It could be something you care about, or it could be something that's essentially irrelevant.

Keep it straightforward. The more up front you are, the more likely the person will trust you, which might increase the likelihood of cooperation. Of course, there will be certain situations in which there will be an inherent lack of trust. In our combined decades of experience as polygraph examiners, we can assure you that we never had a person walk into the room and tell us how happy and excited he was to be there. The best we could hope for was that at some point, the individual would say something like "For a polygraph examiner, you're not too bad." Coming across as sincere and straightforward helps a lot in getting to that point.

emphasis whatsoever placed on the question.

There's another reason that neutrality is especially important. You want to ensure that if there's a deceptive response to the question, the deceptive behavior is related to your question, and not to your delivery. If the person has decided to be untruthful, deceptive behavior tends to be amplified in response to presumptive and bait questions. These questions also tend to be effective in compelling the person to think about changing his game plan, and perhaps to provide you with some information. The original game plan might have been to say, "No, I didn't do it, and I don't know anything about it." Now, in response to the question about what happened at Nicole's last night, Simpson may still want to say he didn't do it, but he may be thinking about what he could share that might make himself appear to be more cooperative. If the person gets into the mode of wanting to share something, that will often open the door to allow you to explore other pieces of information.

"WHAT ELSE?"

Possibly the most important phrase in the information-collection process is the simple question, "What else?" Those two words convey to the person you're interviewing a sense that being selective about the information he shares with you will be no easy task. They also serve as a great example of just how crucial follow-up questions can be. Another great example is asking for a clarification. If the person says anything that you're not absolutely clear about, don't proceed to the next question without clarifying it. It might be something as simple as an acronym you're not familiar with. If you don't know, ask, because you may not have the opportunity to ask later.

To give you a sense of how powerful presumptive questions are, to this day Phil recalls the very first time he used one. It was in the first screening interview he ever conducted—the subject was a male nurse we'll call "Tom," who had been dismissed from his last job at a hospital under suspicion of having stolen controlled substances. On the floor where Tom worked, there were repeated instances of missing drugs, sparking an investigation that found Tom to be the most likely culprit. Throughout the investigation Tom had denied any involvement, and now he was applying for a position at a new hospital. Tom's background and behavior led Phil to suspect that he hadn't been truthful in the investigation, so Phil decided to open the interview not by asking Tom if he had stolen any of the missing drugs, but by posing a presumptive question: "Of all the missing drugs, how many did you take from the hospital?"

There was a long pause—Tom was clearly processing the question. He was

The ability to recognize when and how to follow up on a question can, in fact, make or break an interview. Here are some key types of follow-up questions that you should always have in your interviewing arsenal:

Evaluation
Used to test the information the person has shared

"Why do you say that?"

"How do you know that to be true?"

"On what do you base that information?"

Exploration
Used to acquire additional information

"What else?"

"Tell me more."

"I don't understand."

likely thinking to himself, "What have they discovered that this guy knows about?" In the end, there was no further elicitation required. Phil just sat there and waited patiently, and Tom ultimately decided to share the fact that he had stolen most of the drugs.

For Phil, a key takeaway from that encounter was the sense that what helped to make the presumptive question successful was that he had delivered it in a very low-key, matter-of-fact manner. As a result, Tom wasn't offended—there was no umbrage taken. We've found that if deceptive people do express anger or indignation in response to a presumptive question, it's usually feigned as a strategy to get the questioner to back off. Truthful people typically aren't offended, either, because they recognize that you're just doing your job. So you shouldn't be reluctant to ask those questions, as long as you deliver them in a low-key, neutral way.

Now, what if Tom had not confessed? Phil's next question would have been a bait: "Is there any reason that any new information about your involvement with the missing drugs might have surfaced since you left that job?" This would likely have fleshed out what Tom's game plan might be. If his response to the presumptive question had been something like, "As I told the investigators, I had nothing to do with it," that would tell Phil that Tom's game plan was to stick with what had worked for him during the investigation. One goal of the bait question would be to get him to change that game plan.

There are many different question types available to us, but for our purpose here we'll focus on those that are most helpful as we put the model into practice. With presumptive and bait questions afforded their due, let's examine some of those other key question types.

We often hear that the best questions to ask are *open-ended questions*, and the worst are *closed-ended questions*. The reason, we're told, is that open-ended questions enable us to collect a steady stream of information, while closed-ended questions limit the flow to a single drop of

Clarification
Used to ensure that you're absolutely clear about what the person has shared

"Which 'Sam' are you referring to?"

"Tell me again what time you left."

"Is it possible you were there longer?"

QUESTION TYPES

Open-ended
Provides the basis for discussion or explores an issue

"Tell me what you did yesterday after you arrived at the office."

Closed-ended
Probes specific case facts

"Did you log on to Shelly's computer yesterday?"

Presumptive
Presumes that something is understood to be the case

"What computers on the network have you logged on to besides your own?"

Bait
Establishes a hypothetical situation to trigger a "mind virus"

"If we were to ask your coworkers, is there any reason any of them would say they saw you sitting at Shelly's computer yesterday?"

information. But does that inherently make open-ended questions better?

Suppose we were to put some cash into an envelope, and tell you that you can have the cash if you can ascertain the amount by asking us as many questions as you'd like. The only catch is, you can only ask open-ended questions; no closed-ended questions allowed. You'll find that you can ask open-ended questions from now till the cows come home, but you'll eventually give up in exasperation.

The fact is, no single question type is necessarily the best—it depends entirely on the situation and the particular information you're trying to collect. Open-ended questions are most useful when we need to gather information that's going to be used as the foundation for the discussion. And to be most effective, they require an additional step.

Let's imagine that you're a police officer, and you're called to the scene of an automobile accident. You arrive at the scene, and you see that two cars have collided in an intersection—one belongs to Dan and the other belongs to Dana. Dan and Dana are nose to nose, screaming at each other. So you separate them and pull Dana aside first. You need some basic information to work with, and that's what an open-ended question will provide. So your first question might be, "What happened?"

"I was coming up Main Street, and when I got to the intersection, the light was red, and I stopped," Dana says. "After about twenty seconds the light turned green and I proceeded into the intersection, and this guy came from out of nowhere and creamed my car."

Now, since you need this information to work with, you want it to be as solid as it can possibly be. So, you want to reach inside Dana's narrative answer and identify something important—ideally, the most important thing she said—and test it. The best way to do that is to use a closed-ended question, one that will provide specific case facts. In this case, the most important piece

Opinion
Helps to determine how a person feels about a particular issue

"What do you think about the new internal controls the company has implemented?"

Catch-all
Uncovers lies of omission, serves as a safety net

"What haven't I asked you that you think I should know about?"

QUESTIONS TO AVOID

Negative
Asking a negative question conveys to the person your willingness to accept "no," and to perhaps even expect it.

"You don't know Shelly's password, do you?"

Compound
If your question has multiple parts, you often can't be certain which part of the question is triggering the deceptive behavior. Compound questions also give the person the opportunity

to answer just one part, so you need to be alert to the fact that at least one of your questions went unanswered. That can be difficult if the person gives you an exhaustive response to just one part of the question.

"What time did you arrive yesterday, and how long were you there?"

Vague

A vague question allows for excessive latitude in the response. The person can take his answer anywhere he wants to avoid being of any help to you.

"Can you give me some of your thoughts about what's going on?"

of information is probably what color the light was when she entered the intersection. You ask that closed-ended question, and Dana responds, "I told you already. It was green. I've been driving for twenty years, and I've never had an accident." You got a referral statement and two convincing statements. It was a spy-the-lie moment, and you know you have more work to do with Dana.

Always ensure that you're in L-squared mode when you ask those questions. In the case of a closed-ended question, the response can come very quickly, and if you can catch that flash of deception, it can be enormously valuable to you. So keep in mind that there's nothing wrong with these closed-ended questions. When used properly, they don't reduce the flow of information. They enhance it.

Another question type that's important in the information-collection process is the *opinion question*. We discussed an example of an especially useful opinion question in chapter 9, when we examined the Punishment Question: "What do you think should happen to the person who did this?" When you ask a person for his opinion, always use the model to assess his response. It can help you determine whether the person really believes the opinion he's expressing.

The final question type that we want to highlight is the *catch-all question*, which is designed to uncover lies of omission, and also serves as a safety net in the event that you overlooked an issue. There are two points in an interview where you should consider asking a catch-all question. You might ask one to wrap up the discussion about a particular topic of interest within the interview. "What haven't we discussed that we should talk about regarding your relationship with this person?" The second point is at the end of the interview, where you cast a wide net to capture any information that might be relevant but that has not yet surfaced: "What haven't we discussed that's important for me to know about?" Remember Susan's experience with the job applicant who was drugging his wife in order to satisfy his foot fetish? You never know what's lurking in a person's thoughts that a catch-all question might eventually uncover.

11.

Managing Deception to Gain the Advantage

He who permits himself to tell a lie once, finds it much easier to do it a second and third time, till at length it becomes habitual.

—Thomas Jefferson

When Detective Vannatter switched on the tape recorder in that police interrogation room in Parker Center, a cat-and-mouse game began. Who had the advantage? Was it the haggard man with the suspicious cut on his hand, or the two seasoned police detectives who had already gathered enough evidence to obtain a warrant to search the man's home? It might seem somewhat counterintuitive that the advantage rested squarely with O. J. Simpson. But the reason is simple enough. And it's a reality that defines any deception-detection situation you'll find yourself in.

The plain truth is that the person you're questioning starts off with an inherent advantage over you, because he's the one with the information—he already knows what you need to know, but don't. As you position yourself for the cat-and-mouse game you'll play to gain the advantage, you'll be aided immensely by a psychological concept that we call a "cliff moment." When you're requesting information from someone, and he has information he doesn't want to share with you, often what he's saying to himself is, "I can tell them this, this, and this, but I can't tell them all of that, because if I told them all of that, I would suffer consequences." It's the equivalent of him standing on the edge of a cliff—if he takes one more step, he's a goner. So he says to himself, "I can only tell them up to here."

As he formulates his game plan, you need to formulate yours in a way that helps you prevent what behavioral psychologists call "psychological entrenchment."

When you sit down to interview an individual, he likely has come into the interview with some idea of what he wants to say, and has reasons for wanting to say it. If the truthful response to your question is "yes," and he says, "no," he has lied, and he has a reason for doing so. If the person is put in a position of having to respond to the question again, the psychological entrenchment begins; he's forced to dig his heels in and repeat the lie, otherwise he's exposed as a liar. Every time you allow the deceptive person to verbalize the lie in response to your hammering on the question, his entrenchment deepens, and his advantage rises. You may think you're influencing or encouraging the person to come clean, but you're more likely to be shooting yourself in the foot. The more times you allow him to say "no," the easier it typically will get for him to say it.

Approaching an interview with a cynical, "If your lips are moving, you must be lying" mind-set would get you nowhere. What we can say, though, is that if the person is lying, you don't want his lips moving—you want to provide as little opportunity as possible for him to engage in deception. In cases where you are faced with deception, though, you need to be able to manage it. Let's look at some techniques that you can incorporate into your interviewing style and approach to do that, and to gain the advantage in your encounter.

AVOID ASKING NEGATIVE QUESTIONS. There's no getting around the fact that we all ask negative questions, and sometimes we ask them instinctively. In situations where we don't get the response we expect, we often go into the negative question mode. Suppose you ask a person if she's ever driven above the speed limit, and she responds, "No, never." That's probably a surprising response, so your natural reaction might be to say, "You've never driven above the speed limit? Never?" Keep in mind that once a person commits to a response, that sort of reaction is likely to make psychological entrenchment unavoidable.

USE PROLOGUES FOR KEY QUESTIONS. A prologue is a short, narrative explanation that precedes a question. It's designed to prime the information pump, so that if the person is on the fence about whether or not he's going to give you something, it will help to influence him to come down on your side of the fence. A question prologue might sound something like this:

The next thing I need to ask you about is drug use. Now, before we get into that, let me explain why it's important that we ask this question, and what we're looking for. First of all, we know that a lot of folks have tried things. That's not a particular concern to us. What we are worried about is if someone has a significant drug problem.

There are several elements that can be included in this mini-monologue. One key element is a legitimacy statement—an explanation that asking the questions is an important step in the accomplishment of a resolution. It might seem surprising that the simple act of telling the person that asking the questions is important would increase the odds that he will be more responsive and cooperative. But there is a fascinating human behavior at work here.

In his book, *Influence: The Psychology of Persuasion*, Arizona State University professor Robert Cialdini wrote about automatic response patterns, and how common those patterns are in hu-

> **QUESTION PROLOGUE ELEMENTS**
>
> - Legitimacy statement
> - Rationalization
> - Minimization
> - Projection of blame

man behavior. He cited an experiment in which people standing in line to use a photocopier were approached by individuals with requests to butt in line. If the person making the request gave the reason that he was in a rush, he was successful 94 percent of the time. If no reason was given, the success rate dropped to 60 percent. What was remarkable is that when a person gave a reason that was essentially meaningless—"because I have to make some copies"—the success rate jumped back up to 93 percent. So people respond to legitimacy statements, even if those statements lack a great deal of substance.

Rationalization is also valuable in a question prologue. A socially acceptable reason for an action, like "Nobody's perfect," or "Everyone makes mistakes," can have a tremendous impact on a person's willingness to open up in response to a question.

Similarly, minimization can be an effective tool in preventing psychological entrenchment, so a statement like "No one wants to blow this out of proportion"

STAY COOL

Dealing with deceptive behavior can often be frustrating, and depending on the circumstances, it can be downright infuriating. But you need to stay cool, because taking a non-confrontational approach is always the way to go when you're confronted with deception. Here are some examples of specific behaviors and how we suggest you handle them:

Convincing statements. As we explained in chapter 6, the best strategy for dealing with convincing statements is to neutralize them—you acknowledge or agree with them, and go right back to where you were in the questioning process.

Exclusion qualifiers. When a person uses an exclusion qualifier like "not really," "for the most part," or "basically," her aim is to provide you with an answer, but to carve out information that she doesn't want to share. When you hear one of those qualifiers, your very next question should be targeted at what has potentially been carved out. Let's say a couple is getting dressed to go out. The husband picks out a shirt and asks his wife if she has any problem with his choice, and she says, "Not really." If the husband shoots back with "What is 'not really' supposed to mean?" aside from the stage being set for a less-than-enjoyable evening, she's likely to minimize what she otherwise might have

might be helpful. At the same time, it's crucial that the person not be misled with false information. If the discussion centers around activity that is criminal in nature, for example, there must be no inference that the activity is not a crime.

A final element that might be included in a question prologue is a projection of blame. In an investigation of inappropriate accounting activity in a company, for instance, this projection of blame might be conveyed something like this: "Sometimes the real problem here is that we don't take enough time to explain to folks what the right procedures are. And as a result of that, sometimes crazy things happen."

Remember, don't overuse question prologues. Reserve them for key questions when discussing the most important topics.

OVERCOME PSYCHOLOGICAL ALIBIS. It can be quite frustrating to hear, in response to a question, "I don't remember," or "Not that I recall." As we pointed out in chapter 5, selective memory is a problem, because if it's an alibi, it's a tough alibi to crack. A person's inability to remember something can obviously be legitimate, and depending on the question, a statement like "Not to my knowledge" can well be the most appropriate truthful response.

If, by applying the model, you have reason to believe that the person is using a statement like this as a means of withholding information, it's essential to avoid creating that psychological entrenchment. Your natural inclination might be to ask, "How could you possibly be unable to remember something like that?" But in doing so, you'd be forcing the person to dig in his heels and stand firm. What you need to do instead is compel him to change his game plan.

A very effective way to do that is to follow up with a bait question. If we hear an "I don't remember" in response to a question, say, about whether a person had ever met a particular individual, we might follow up with, "Is there any reason anyone might tell us that he saw the two of you together?"

shared if he had been more low-key. If he really wants to know what she thinks (granted, the chances of that may be slim), he's much better off coming back with something like, "If you had to pick out one thing about this shirt that you're not crazy about, what would it be?"

Inconsistent statements. If a person's response to a question is inconsistent with something he said previously, your inclination might be to come back with something like, "Wait a minute! That's not what you said before!" But if you do that, how cooperative is he likely to be? The person has provided you with information that might be closer to the truth than what he said earlier, and he doesn't want his nose rubbed in the fact that he didn't share it with you previously.

If a person says the amount of money he stole is $500, and later in the interview says the amount is $1,000, you don't want the next thing out of your mouth to be, "That's not what you said before." A better way to resolve the conflict and evaluate the truthfulness of the update often is to follow up with a question about whether there's another possibility, such as, "Is it possible that it could have been more than $1,000 that you took?" It can also be helpful to follow up with a question that's preceded by a legitimacy statement: "I just want to make

Another strategy that often works well is the "possibility strategy." An example might be "I know it was a while ago, but is it possible that the two of you might have met?" There are no guarantees here, but people often recognize the conundrum you're putting them in: It's often nonsensical to claim that something is impossible. So, if you're able to cross that first hurdle by getting the person to acknowledge it's possible, you might continue to use the possibility strategy, or you may be able to shift it to reality: "Okay, what do you remember about that meeting?"

BROADEN YOUR FOCUS. Another powerful tactic you might use as a means of increasing the volume of useful information you collect, and one you should use routinely, is to broaden your focus in a way that makes it more difficult for the person to give you a narrow response. If the person has made the decision to go into deceptive mode, his mission is to get you to believe something that's contrary to the reality of the situation. By broadening your area of focus in a particular line of questioning, you can steer him off of that path and onto one that gives you additional information.

When we conducted screening interviews at the CIA, one of the questions we would ask was "Have you ever used any illegal drugs?" Often, we would get a response like, "I experimented with marijuana one time." Upon getting that response, your inclination might be to follow up with questions that accept that thesis: "When was that?" or "Who was that with?" But the problem you create for yourself when you do that is that you set yourself up for more resistance and for more psychological entrenchment. You want to get the person to tell you the real story, and do it in a way that enables you to pursue the information without becoming the adversary.

Broadening your focus allows you to explore what's on the other side of that cliff we talked about—what's in the ravine, or what's beyond the line in the sand that the individual has drawn. To do that, you first need to be clear on what the original thesis was: "I experimented

sure—if I understand correctly, we're talking about $1,000." If you need to compare and contrast the new statement with the previous statement, do it, but don't beat the person up over it—your aim is to solicit his cooperation: "Okay, now how does that fit with what you said before? Help me understand how we got from there to here." Make sure you're in L-squared mode, using the model every step of the way.

with marijuana one time." Resist the urge to go after that. You have that piece of information, and you can always explore it. Instead, what you want to do is broaden your focus to explore the possibility of more extensive use of illegal drugs. An effective way to do that is to ask a presumptive question: "Okay, what other things have you tried?" or "When was the last time you experimented?" What you're doing, in a professional, nonconfrontational way, is nudging the person psychologically to see where he might go.

Once you've obtained a series of information pieces, explore them in reverse order. The reason is simple: The last piece of information the person gave you is likely to be the most serious piece, the one he was most reluctant to share. The bottom line is that you don't accept the first thing someone tells you. It's almost as if you didn't hear it.

12.

Let's Be Careful Out There

Truth only reveals itself when one gives up all
preconceived ideas.

—*Japanese proverb*

The TV crime drama *Lie to Me*, which aired on the Fox network from January 2009 to January 2011, exposed a huge worldwide audience to the field of deception detection. The main character, Dr. Cal Lightman, played masterfully by British film actor Tim Roth, was an expert in identifying and interpreting microexpressions—involuntary facial movements that can reflect various emotions. Dr. Lightman would spot one of these movements on the face of a bad guy, and proclaim with dramatic flair that the bad guy was lying.

That, of course, was Hollywood, and it certainly didn't do justice to some of the great research that has been done in the realm of microexpressions. These split-second facial movements, which can reflect emotions as varied as fear, anger, contempt, rage, guilt, shame, and disgust, can be extremely valuable in revealing what a person might really be thinking in a given situation. If a person appears on the surface to be calm and collected, but we can spot microexpressions that reflect an underlying level of anxiety, that can be very useful information.

However, in the field of deception detection, microexpressions have two significant limitations. First, there is no specific microexpression for deception. A microexpression that is associated with anxiety, for example, *could* be an indicator of deception, depending on the stimulus. But in isolation, the reliability of that indicator may be quite low. Any conclusion about the meaning of the microexpression therefore becomes a matter of guesswork.

The second limitation of microexpressions is their impracticality. Unless you're very highly trained and are able to develop the uncanny sharpness of focus that would enable you to spot a facial movement that lasts a fraction of a second, it's not a pragmatic tool to reach for in a typical, real-time encounter. So the Lightman-esque routine of staring into someone's face and determining that the person is lying makes for good TV, but that's where it's best left.

We would put microexpressions in a category of behaviors that have come to be widely viewed as reliable indicators of deception, but that we in our experience have found to more typically be quite unreliable in real situations. Here are some other behaviors that we advise be used with extreme care, and that we lump into a category we think of as "Behavioral Cautions."

EYE CONTACT. If you ask ten people to give you a list of five behaviors that are reliable indicators of deception, don't be surprised if all ten mention a failure to have good eye contact. Most of them would likely be unable to tell you how or why they came to understand that there is a connection between eye contact and deception; it's just one of those things that, for whatever reason, seems to be generally accepted. Our advice is, don't accept it. Yes, poor eye contact may be bad manners in a lot of situations, depending on the culture. But let's face it—the leap from there to deception requires a pretty long running start.

Let's say we're talking to someone, and suddenly, at a critical moment, she breaks eye contact; she looks to the side, or looks down. What should we conclude from that? Is it a feeling of discomfort? Is it a reflection of a heightened degree of anxiety? Is there an issue related to a lack of self-confidence or self-esteem? Is there a lack of social sophistication or comfort? Is she unable to look at you because she's about to lie to you? It could be any of those things, because eye contact is a highly individualistic behavior. Eye contact as a behavior can't be applied universally, moreover, because the behavior varies from culture to culture, not only in different countries, but in different regions within the same country.

Beyond all that, how much time do we really spend looking

into each other's eyes? Consider what prolonged eye contact between two people signals: It's a message that's most typically conveyed either at a time of intimacy, or at a time of challenge—two diametrically opposing situations. That tells you that precisely the same behavior can signal two completely opposite messages. So we need to be extremely careful in trying to interpret what any eye activity really means.

CLOSED POSTURE. The idea that a closed posture is a deceptive behavior has some merit, because an isolated logical point can be associated with it. If a person doesn't want to cooperate, that may be equivalent to shutting down, and a closed posture is seen as a sign of a shutdown. But there's a problem with making a sweeping judgment on the basis of that isolated logical point. Remember in chapter 2, when we talked about global behavior assessment? We noted that closed posture is a great example of a global behavior that puts you in a position of having to guess why it's being exhibited. Is it because the person is cold, or because he's just comfortable sitting that way? Since you don't know, you can't rely on it, so you can't make a decision on that basis. You can't attach significance to a behavior if you don't know its cause.

GENERAL NERVOUS TENSION. Law enforcement operations for years have associated a heightened level of anxiety with deception. True enough, we know there is a connection between anxiety and deception. But if we simply look at anxiety globally, it's much like closed posture—we can only guess at the cause of the nervousness. Is she nervous because she's lying, because she's the one who committed the wrongdoing? Is she nervous because she's never been interviewed by a police officer before, or because there's a peripheral issue, like she suspects a particular individual of committing the wrongdoing? Is there a medical issue that creates an appearance of nervousness? Is she simply nervous by nature? Who really knows?

PREEMPTIVE RESPONSES. Responding to a question before the questioner has finished asking it is sometimes considered to be indicative of deceptive behavior. We don't accept that. Our experience has demonstrated that this is a behavior routinely exhibited by both truthful and deceptive people, but they do so for different reasons. The truthful person is dying to get the fact that he didn't do it out on the table. He's not thinking about giving you a preemptive response. The facts are his ally, and he wants you to know it as soon as possible. Conversely, the deceptive person is in the extremely uncomfortable position of dealing with a situation in which the facts are not his ally. He's made up his mind that he's going to lie, and he just wants to get it out there and get it over with as soon as possible.

BLUSHING OR TWITCHING. These involuntary behaviors may be caused by anxiety, but they're just as likely to be caused by something else—perhaps it's neurological, temperature-related, or medication-related. Blushing, moreover, reflects emotions that can have nothing to do with lying. The person might simply be embarrassed by the question or by the topic. So these behaviors have proven to be not nearly as definitive as those we've equipped you with in the model.

CLENCHED HANDS. This behavior is typically seen as a deceptive indicator in the law-enforcement community, where it's commonly referred to as "white knuckles"—the person is so scared and so tense that he doesn't even realize his hands are clenched so tightly that the blood has rushed away from his knuckles and they've turned white. But once again, this is a global behavior. When it doesn't occur as a direct, timely response to a stimulus, you can only guess at the significance of the behavior. Yes, it may well be an indication that the person is scared, but you have no way of knowing what's causing it. Is he afraid because he's intimidated by authority figures? Is he afraid that no one will believe him? Is it because he's being deceptive? It's a roll of the dice.

BASELINING. The theory behind baselining is that we can ask a person control questions to which we know the answers, and capture what the person looks and sounds like when he responds truthfully. Then, with that baseline, if there's an aberration from that behavior in response to the other questions we ask, that's an indicator that those answers may be untruthful. It's a reasonable approach because we humans really like to compare things. It's an extension of why we love analogy—it helps us make sense of complicated issues, and it makes our lives easier. But when we engage in baselining, we run into a couple of problems.

First, it's simple faulty logic to assume that whatever it is a person is doing differently is indicative of deception. It's not a leap that can reliably be made, because human beings are too complicated, and the ocean of emotions and behaviors that a person can conceivably exhibit is far too vast for such a comparison to tell us anything that's truly meaningful.

Second, the fact is people are smart enough, and it's certainly easy enough, to game the baselining system. An arsonist who burned down a school knows that he's going to be asked difficult questions, and that coming up with answers that he hopes will enable him to avoid suffering any consequences will take some time. So when he's asked a control question such as, "When were you born?" he may be thinking far enough ahead to repeat the question or make a nonanswer statement, because he knows he'll have to do that to buy himself some time when he's asked the tough questions. Beyond that, on a more subtle level, the person isn't going to wait for the "Did you set fire to the school?" question to try to start convincing you of his innocence. If you ask him what his job is, he may launch into a lengthy explanation of what he does and why it's so important. Every word of it may be true, but his aim is to convince you that he wants to be cooperative, that he's perfectly willing to engage with you, and that he's not afraid of the situation. Then when the "Did you do it?" question comes, he launches into a series of convincing statements: "I pay taxes to build our schools"; "I have friends whose kids go to that school"; "I'm a respected member of the community." You draw the conclusion that this is just the way the guy answers questions. And you just got beat.

There's another dimension to baselining that can get you into trouble, as well. The idea here is that you have some basic concept of how people who fit into a particular demographic typically act in a given situation, and you consider that as a baseline. If a person in that demographic acts in a manner that departs significantly from the parameters of the norm that's been established as the baseline, then we have a red flag that suggests the person is being deceptive. Those are very dangerous waters to tread in, because lying is not a team sport—it's very individualistic. So both truthful and deceptive people might exhibit behaviors that don't conform to an expected norm. Let's look at an example that demonstrates what we mean.

A seventeen-year-old female who had enrolled in the Police Explorers, a national program aimed at encouraging youth to get involved in community service and auxiliary police operations, mentioned to the female dispatcher at a local police department that she had engaged in a sex act with one of the officers on the force. Little did she know that the dispatcher was dating that particular officer. Not surprisingly, the dispatcher was livid, and she immediately reported the incident to the police chief. The officer, who was well liked and highly regarded on the force, strongly denied the incident, and everyone from the police chief on down—and even the girl's father—suspected that the girl had fabricated the story. After she was questioned, they were convinced she was indeed making it all up because she had shown no signs of being upset or ashamed. Since she exhibited none of the shame or emotional discomfort that the investigators were convinced would characterize the behavior of any teenage girl in her position, her demeanor told the investigators that she had to be lying. It wasn't until Michael was brought in to interview the girl and the officer that the case was resolved. After questioning the girl, he was convinced that she was telling the truth. So when he questioned the officer, his aim was to elicit a confession. Within the course of a single interview, the officer admitted to Michael that he had indeed engaged in the sex act with the girl.

13.

A Textbook Case of Deception

Truth fears no questions.

—Unknown

One of the biggest national news stories in the United States in the spring of 2011, was the scandal surrounding the sexting activities of Congressman Anthony Weiner of New York. In the span of ten days, Weiner went from staunchly, defiantly, and repeatedly denying that he had sent a lewd photo of himself to a female college student on Twitter, to a tearful public admission that he not only sent that photo, but he had engaged in similar inappropriate activity with six women over a period of three years.

The Weiner episode warrants examination here because it serves as a textbook case study of many of the deceptive behaviors we have presented in these pages. To set the stage, here's a brief timeline of the events that took place during that ten-day span:

May 27: Weiner sent the lewd photo via Twitter to a female college student in Seattle. He had intended to send it as a direct tweet that only she would see, but soon realized he had inadvertently sent it on his open Twitter feed. He deleted it and tweeted a claim that his account had been hacked.

May 28: BigGovernment.com reported that Weiner sent the lewd photo, which showed a man's underwear-clad crotch area.

May 29: A Weiner spokesman said the lewd photograph sent from the congressman's Twitter account was the work of a hacker, and dismissed it as a "distraction."

May 31: Weiner spoke with a group of reporters who had gathered outside his Capitol Hill office, but declined to answer their questions about the photo.

June 1: Weiner did a series of TV interviews in which he steadfastly denied that he had sent the lewd photo, but said he was unable to say "with certitude" whether the photo was of him.

June 6: BigGovernment.com published shirtless photos of Weiner provided by a second woman. Weiner convened a press conference in Manhattan to announce that he had sent the photo to the female college student, that he had repeatedly lied about it to protect himself and his wife, and that he had had inappropriate online exchanges with six women.

Now, let's slip another date in there: June 2. That's the day—four days before Weiner finally confessed—that we posted our analysis of the case on *The True Verdict* Web site, in which we drew this conclusion:

His behavior suggests it's probably much more than tweeting a single lewd photo to a female college student. It's more likely that he's trying to conceal a pattern of this type of behavior, which would suggest he has possibly been following this young woman for some time, and likely other young women as well. It also strongly suggests that this is not the only photo of this type that has been sent by Weiner.

What was it that enabled us to arrive at that conclusion? Simple. We applied the model to an analysis of the transcript of that May 31 exchange that Weiner had with reporters outside his office. Now it's your turn.

Below is the full transcript of that exchange, which was reported on by multiple media outlets. Weiner exhibited over sixty deceptive behaviors in this single encounter with

reporters. Read through it, and see how many you can identify. We'll show you what we spotted, and what led us to
draw our conclusion, later in the chapter.

The main characters in the exchange with Weiner were
Dana Bash, senior congressional correspondent for CNN; and
Ted Barrett, CNN's senior congressional producer.

Bash: Congressman, can you just answer point-blank?
You say that you were hacked, which is potentially a
crime. So why haven't you asked the Capitol Police or
any law enforcement to investigate?

Weiner: Look, this was a prank that I've now been
talking about for a couple of days. I'm not going to allow it to decide what I talk about for the next week or
the next two weeks, and so I'm not going to give you
anything more about that today. I think I've been pretty
responsive to you in the past.

Bash: But with respect, you're here, which we appreciate, but you're not answering the questions. Can you
just say why you haven't asked law enforcement to investigate what you are alleging is a crime?

Weiner: You know, Dana, if I was giving a speech to
forty-five thousand people and someone in the back of

the room threw a pie or yelled out an insult, would I spend the next two hours responding to that? No. I would get back . . .

Barrett (*interrupting*): This is not that situation.

Weiner: You want to do the briefing?

Barrett: You said from your Twitter account, a lewd photo was sent to a college student. Answer the question. Was it from you or not?

Weiner: Sir, permit me to . . . Do you guys want me to finish my answer?

Barrett: Yes, this answer. Did you send it or not?

Weiner: Okay. If I were giving a speech to forty-five thousand people and someone in the back threw a pie or yelled out an insult, I would not spend the next two hours of my speech responding to that pie or that insult. I would return to the things that I want to talk about to the audience that I want to talk to, and that is what I intend to do this week.

Barrett: All you would have to do is say "no."

Bash: Let me try this question: The woman who allegedly got this tweet, or it was directed to, a twenty-one-year-old college student in Seattle, she released a statement to the *New York Daily News* yesterday saying you follow her on Twitter. Is that true? Did you follow her on Twitter? And if so, how did you find her? What was the reason?

Weiner: You know, I have, I think, said this a couple of ways, and I'll say it again. I am not going to permit myself to be distracted by this issue any longer.

Barrett: All you have to do is say "no" to that question.

Weiner: You are free . . . Why don't you let me do the answers and you do the questions?

Barrett: If you would answer the question asked you, sir, we will.

Unidentified reporter: You follow an awful lot of young women on Twitter. Is there a reason you have so many ladies that you're following?

Weiner: By the way, in related news, I have in the famous hashtag "ScrappyChasingCrazy," I passed Michele Bachmann today in the number of Twitter followers. I will give you that additional fact.

Bash: You can understand what's going on here, the frustration. We appreciate you coming out here talking to us—you're smiling, you're cooperating, and that's good offense. But you're not answering the questions . . .

Weiner: This is now Day Three. You have statements that my office has put out.

Bash: But they don't answer the questions . . .

Weiner: There are statements that my office put out and there are going to be people who are going to want . . . Look, this is the tactic. The guy in the back of the room who's throwing the pie or yelling out the insult wants that to be the conversation.

Bash: But you're the one who said you were hacked . . .

Weiner: Dana, let me . . . I have to ask that we follow some rules here, and one of them is going to be you ask the questions and I give the answers. Does that seem reasonable?

Bash: I'd love to get an answer.

Weiner: That would be reasonable . . .

Barrett: Direct answer.

Weiner: That would be reasonable. You do the questions, I do the answers and this jackass [referring to Barrett] interrupts me. How about that as the new rule of the game? Let me just give the answer. The objective of the person who is doing the mischief is to try to distract me from what I'm doing. So, for the last couple of days that has happened. I've made a decision. I'm not going to let it happen today. I'm not going to let it happen tomorrow. You're doing your job, I understand it. Just go ahead and do it, but you're going to have to do it without me, every day, answering questions about this. Today, I want to talk about the debt limit vote. This debt limit vote tonight is a very important . . .

Barrett: Congressman, why haven't you asked the police to investigate this? Why did you not ask the police to investigate this? Is it because you don't want them to find out what the answer is?

Weiner: Let me make a point about the debt limit. You know, we are tonight at 6:30, 6:45, going to be casting a vote on something that has monumental importance to our economy, whether or not we have a stunt vote on something as important as the debt limit. I want to focus what I talk about on that. I want to focus what I'm working on, on that. I want to focus on that because frankly, I think my constituents want me to, and I think that frankly, the country would want me to. So, that's what I'm going to do. You don't have to. You can continue doing whatever you want to do. But I am not going to allow this thing to dominate what I talk about any further.

Bash: In the statements you put out, you said that you were hacked. It's sort of a logical question that we really wish that you would answer. Why, if you were the victim of a crime . . .

Weiner: You've got to refer to my statements. You've got to refer to my statements.

Bash: The statements don't answer the question. If they did, we'd be happy to. The statements don't answer the question.

Weiner: All I can tell you is I put out statements the last couple of days, responding to everyone saying, "This is the last question we're going to ask." And in fact, it's pretty clear that by your presence here, some people have been successful in making the conversation about something I simply choose not to participate in anymore. You can feel free to still cover it . . .

Barrett *(interrupting)*: Congressman, you would deny this . . . you would answer directly . . .

Weiner: You can be here, and you can feel free to stay here and ask me again. But you know, we have a situation where across the way is the Supreme Court, that Justice Clarence Thomas, his household received over $800,000 of remuneration from people that are trying to overturn the health care law, trying to stop it, and yet he's refusing to recuse himself. I think that's pretty important. That's an important thing that I'm going to devote my energies to, and those are the things I'm going to talk about.

Unidentified reporter: Your statement did say that you did retain a lawyer, so what are you directing your attorney to do on your behalf? Ask for an investigation?

Weiner: I think the statement speaks to that. It says they are going to advise us on appropriate next steps. . . . I would refer you back to the statement and read it in its entirety.

Barrett: Who is the attorney?

Weiner: Are there any other questions? Look, there are people who are going to want to try to distract from the work that I have to do. There are. There are going to be people who are going to want to have this debate. And to some degree, the people that are engaging it are zealous to do it. Why? But I don't want to. I choose to fight for the things that I care about, and the things that I'm working on. Look, can I tell you something? I know this is how the game is played. Some people decide they want to talk about this thing for days and days. I choose not to. That's my prerogative. I'm sorry. Sorry.

Bash: Can I just throw this out there, though? If this is the nonstory that you say this is, and a distraction . . .

Weiner (*interrupting*): I didn't characterize it . . . I characterized it as a distraction. I'll leave it to you to make the decision of whether it's a story.

Bash: If you think this is just a distraction, you're a sophisticated guy. Why not just answer the questions, and then you'll be done with it?

Weiner: I've been doing that for several days. Now I choose . . . There are people who apparently haven't read the statements. I assume that you have. Look, all I can tell you is this: This is akin to someone deciding on Day Three or Day Four they want to continue talking about something that I consider a distraction, and me making a decision on how I'm going to deal with this. And the decision I have made is I'm not going to permit it to distract me. I'm not going to permit it to continue on for three, four, five, or six more days. If that's unsatisfactory to you, I apologize. But I think that what people really want to talk about are things like the debt limit vote tonight. Things like the oppressive disparity between the very well-to-do in this country and people that don't have as much. Or the fact that it's more and more difficult being in the middle class in this country. That's what I'm here to work on. Thank you, guys.

How do you think you did? It's amazing how the behaviors you read about earlier can readily be identified in deceptive people, isn't it? Now, here's the transcript again, with Weiner's deceptive behaviors listed under each of his responses. We've included explanatory notes where they're warranted.

Bash: Congressman, can you just answer point-blank? You say that you were hacked, which is potentially a crime. So why haven't you asked the Capitol Police or any law enforcement to investigate?

Weiner: Look, this was a prank that I've now been talking about for a couple of days. I'm not going to allow it to decide what I talk about for the next week or the next two weeks, and so I'm not going to give you anything more about that today. I think I've been pretty responsive to you in the past.

DECEPTIVE BEHAVIORS

- *Failure to answer the question*

- *Refusal to answer the question*

- *Referral statement—"I think I've been pretty responsive to you in the past."*

- *Two exclusion qualifiers—"I think" and "pretty"*

Bash: But with respect, you're here, which we appreciate, but you're not answering the questions. Can you just say why you haven't asked law enforcement to investigate what you are alleging is a crime?

Weiner: You know, Dana, if I was giving a speech to forty-five thousand people and someone in the back of the room threw a pie or yelled out an insult, would I spend the next two hours responding to that? No. I would get back . . .

DECEPTIVE BEHAVIORS

- *Failure to answer the question*

- *Inappropriate/disconnected question—"If I was giving a speech to forty-five thousand people and someone in the back of the room threw a pie or yelled out an insult, would I spend the next two hours responding to that?"*

Barrett *(interrupting)***:** This is not that situation.

Weiner: You want to do the briefing?

DECEPTIVE BEHAVIOR

- *Attacking the questioner*

Barrett: You said from your Twitter account, a lewd photo was sent to a college student. Answer the question. Was it from you or not?

Weiner: Sir, permit me to . . . Do you guys want me to finish my answer?

DECEPTIVE BEHAVIORS

- *Failure to answer the question*

- *Inappropriate level of politeness—"Sir"*

- *Attacking behavior—Weiner's question intimates that the reporters are being rude and acting inappropriately toward him.*

Barrett: Yes, this answer. Did you send it or not?

Weiner: Okay. If I were giving a speech to forty-five thousand people and someone in the back threw a pie or yelled out an insult, I would not spend the next two hours of my speech responding to that pie or that insult. I would return to the things that I want to talk about to the audience that I want to talk to, and that is what I intend to do this week.

DECEPTIVE BEHAVIORS

- *Failure to answer the question*

- *Nonanswer statements*

There is also an unintended message. With his statement, "I would return to things that I want to talk about," Weiner acknowledges that he doesn't want to talk about this issue, to include responding to reasonable questions.

Barrett: All you would have to do is say "no."

Bash: Let me try this question: The woman who allegedly got this tweet, or it was directed to, a twenty-one-year-old college student in Seattle, she released a statement to the *New York Daily News* yesterday saying you follow her on Twitter. Is that true? Did you follow her on Twitter? And if so, how did you find her? What was the reason?

Weiner: You know, I have, I think, said this a couple of ways, and I'll say it again. I am not going to permit myself to be distracted by this issue any longer.

DECEPTIVE BEHAVIORS

- *Failure to answer the question*

- *Refusal to answer the question*

- *Referral statement*

- *Nonanswer statement*

Barrett: All you have to do is say "no" to that question.

Weiner: You are free . . . Why don't you let me do the answers and you do the questions?

DECEPTIVE BEHAVIOR

- *Attacking the questioner*

Barrett: If you would answer the question asked you, sir, we will.

Unidentified reporter: You follow an awful lot of young women on Twitter. Is there a reason you have so many ladies that you're following?

Weiner: By the way, in related news, I have in the famous hashtag "ScrappyChasingCrazy," I passed Michele Bachmann today in the number of Twitter followers. I will give you that additional fact.

DECEPTIVE BEHAVIORS

- *Failure to answer the question*

- *Nonanswer statements*

- *Inappropriate level of concern (comical response)*

Bash: You can understand what's going on here, the frustration. We appreciate you coming out here talking to us—you're smiling, you're cooperating, and that's good offense. But you're not answering the questions . . .

Weiner: This is now Day Three. You have statements that my office has put out.

DECEPTIVE BEHAVIORS

- *Failure to answer the question*

- *Nonanswer statement*

- *Referral statement*

Bash: But they don't answer the questions . . .

Weiner: There are statements that my office put out and there are going to be people who are going to want . . . look, this is the tactic. The guy in the back of the room who's throwing the pie or yelling out the insult wants that to be the conversation.

DECEPTIVE BEHAVIORS

- *Failure to answer the question*

- *Referral statement*

- *Convincing statement—He's the victim of a "tactic."*

Bash: But you're the one who said you were hacked . . .

Weiner: Dana, let me . . . I have to ask that we follow some rules here, and one of them is going to be you ask the questions and I give the answers. Does that seem reasonable?

DECEPTIVE BEHAVIOR

- *Inappropriate level of politeness*

Bash: I'd love to get an answer.

Weiner: That would be reasonable . . .

Barrett: Direct answer.

Weiner: That would be reasonable. You do the questions, I do the answers and this jackass [referring to Barrett] interrupts me. How about that as the new rule of the game? Let me just give the answer. The objective of the person who is doing the mischief is to try to distract me from what I'm doing. So for the last couple of days that has happened. I've made a decision. I'm not going to let it happen today. I'm not going to let it happen tomorrow. You're doing your job, I understand it. Just go ahead and do it, but you're going to have to do it without me, every day, answering questions about this.

Today, I want to talk about the debt limit vote. This debt limit vote tonight is a very important . . .

DECEPTIVE BEHAVIORS

- *Failure to answer the question*

- *Attacking the questioner*

- *Nonanswer statements*

- *Convincing statements—Intention is to convince us that he's just trying to do his job.*

Barrett: Congressman, why haven't you asked the police to investigate this? Why did you not ask the police to investigate this? Is it because you don't want them to find out what the answer is?

Weiner: Let me make a point about the debt limit. You know, we are tonight at 6:30, 6:45, going to be casting a vote on something that has monumental importance to our economy, whether or not we have a stunt vote on something as important as the debt limit. I want to focus what I talk about on that. I want to focus what I'm working on, on that. I want to focus on that because frankly,

I think my constituents want me to, and I think that frankly, the country would want me to. So, that's what I'm going to do. You don't have to. You can continue doing whatever you want to do. But I am not going to allow this thing to dominate what I talk about any further.

DECEPTIVE BEHAVIORS

- *Failure to answer the question*

- *Refusal to answer the question*

- *Nonanswer statements*

- *Perception qualifiers—Two instances of the word "frankly"*

- *Convincing statements—All he's trying to do is serve his constituents and the country.*

Bash: In the statements you put out, you said that you were hacked. It's sort of a logical question that we really wish that you would answer. Why, if you were the victim of a crime . . .

Weiner: You've got to refer to my statements. You've got to refer to my statements.

DECEPTIVE BEHAVIORS

- *Failure to answer the question*

- *Referral statements*

Bash: The statements don't answer the question. If they did, we'd be happy to. The statements don't answer the question.

Weiner: All I can tell you is I put out statements the last couple of days, responding to everyone saying, "This is the last question we're going to ask." And in fact, it's pretty clear that by your presence here, some people have been successful in making the conversation about something I simply choose not to participate in anymore. You can feel free to still cover it. . . .

DECEPTIVE BEHAVIORS

- *Failure to answer the question*

- *Referral statements*

- *Nonanswer statements*

- *Exclusion qualifier—"All I can tell you . . ." This is also an unintended message that suggests he has information he cannot tell us.*

Barrett *(interrupting)*: Congressman, you would deny this . . . you would answer directly . . .

Weiner: You can be here, and you can feel free to stay here and ask me again. But you know, we have a situation where across the way is the Supreme Court, that Justice Clarence Thomas, his household received over $800,000 of remuneration from people that are trying to overturn the health care law, trying to stop it, and yet he's refusing to recuse himself. I think that's pretty important. That's an important thing that I'm going to devote my energies to, and those are the things I'm going to talk about.

DECEPTIVE BEHAVIORS

- *Failure to answer the question*

- *Nonanswer statements*

- *Convincing statements—He's devoting his energies to serving the cause of justice.*

Unidentified reporter: Your statement did say that you did retain a lawyer, so what are you directing your attorney to do on your behalf? Ask for an investigation?

Weiner: I think the statement speaks to that. It says they are going to advise us on appropriate next steps. . . . I would refer you back to the statement and read it in its entirety.

DECEPTIVE BEHAVIORS

- *Failure to answer the question*

- *Referral statement*

Barrett: Who is the attorney?

Weiner: Are there any other questions? Look, there are people who are going to want to try to distract from the work that I have to do. There are. There are going to be people who are going to want to have this debate. And to some degree, the people that are engaging it are zealous to do it. Why? But I don't want to. I choose to fight for the things that I care about, and the things that I'm working on. Look, can I tell you something? I know this is how the game is played. Some people decide they want to talk about this thing for days and days. I choose not to. That's my prerogative. I'm sorry. Sorry.

DECEPTIVE BEHAVIORS

- *Failure to answer the question*

- *Attacking behavior—"There are people who are going to want to try to distract . . ."*

- *Nonanswer statements*

- *Inappropriate level of politeness—Apologizing*

Bash: Can I just throw this out there, though? If this is the nonstory that you say this is, and a distraction . . .

Weiner (interrupting): I didn't characterize it . . . I characterized it as a distraction. I'll leave it to you to make the decision of whether it's a story.

Bash: If you think this is just a distraction, you're a sophisticated guy. Why not just answer the questions, and then you'll be done with it?

Weiner: I've been doing that for several days. Now I choose . . . there are people who apparently haven't read the statements. I assume that you have. Look, all I can tell you is this: This is akin to someone deciding on Day Three or Day Four they want to continue talking about something that I consider a distraction, and me making a decision on how I'm going to deal with this. And the decision I have made is I'm not going to permit it to distract me. I'm not going to permit it to continue on for three, four, five, or six more days. If that's unsatisfactory to you, I apologize. But I think that what people really want to talk about are things like the debt limit vote tonight. Things like the oppressive disparity between the very well-to-do in this country and people that don't have as much. Or the fact that it's more and more difficult being in the middle class in this country. That's what I'm here to work on. Thank you, guys.

DECEPTIVE BEHAVIORS

- *Failure to answer the question*

- *Refusal to answer the question*

- *Referral statement*

- *Nonanswer statements*

- *Inappropriate level of politeness—Apologizing*

- *Exclusion qualifier—"All I can tell you . . ." Again, this is also an unintended message that there is more he can't tell us.*

- *Attacking behavior—"There are people who apparently haven't read the statements" and "This is akin to someone deciding on Day Three or Day Four they want to continue talking about something I consider a distraction."*

- *Convincing statements—He's championing the fight against such social problems as the disparity between rich and poor.*

Clearly, just about anyone who watched that exchange on CNN could see that Weiner wasn't being forthcoming, and that there had to be a reason that he kept dodging the reporters' questions. That Weiner was being deceptive was obvious. But what, exactly, was he hiding? Was it a one-off event, a foolish aberration that truly didn't warrant the attention it was getting and the distraction it was causing at a time when Congress was dealing with so many crucial issues of vital importance to the American people? Or was it a more serious matter that could potentially create an even more painful distraction in the future? Was there any way to get any informed sense of the degree of the problem at that point? Indeed, there was.

Our analysis of the specific behaviors Weiner exhibited, their frequency and the pattern in which they appeared, led to the conclusion we drew. Here's the full analysis we posted on June 2:

> Weiner exhibited a series of blatant deceptive behaviors that strongly indicate not only that he is being untruthful about this particular matter, but that there is likely much more to the story as it relates to this type of behavior on his part.
>
> The high volume of attack behaviors exhibited by Weiner illustrates his enormously high level of concern, especially when these attacks are made in lieu of answering very direct questions. This level of concern, coupled with his failure to answer any of the questions posed to him, suggests that Weiner finds himself in a very difficult situation. His behavior clearly suggests that he has no facts or information that he wishes to discuss publically on this matter. Those behaviors also indicate that he would rather appear to be obvious in his deception than to let any tidbit of information about his conduct in this area slip out.
>
> When one considers the high value that politicians place on their reputations, it's safe to assume that they would only risk their reputations on something of monumental importance. What is it that's so monumental that

Weiner is risking his reputation to hide? In his responses, Weiner conveys several unintended messages with phrases like "all I can tell you," which suggest that he is concealing behavior that he doesn't want to talk about. His behavior suggests it's probably much more than tweeting a single lewd photo to a female college student. It's more likely that he's trying to conceal a pattern of this type of behavior, which would suggest he has possibly been following this young woman for some time, and likely other young women as well. It also strongly suggests that this is not the only photo of this type that has been sent by Weiner. It would not be surprising to see the "Tiger Woods Phenomenon" unfold here, where other young ladies come out of the woodwork with similar stories.

---

* Source: http://www.cnn.com/#/video/politics/2011/05/31/sot.bash.weiner.twitter.cnn.

† Our analysis: http://truthinthelaw.blogspot.com/2011/06/hot-dog-how-deception-detection-experts.html.

14.

Okay, So Now What?

I never encourage deceit, and falsehood, especially if you have got a bad memory, is the worst enemy a fellow can have. The fact is truth is your truest friend, no matter what the circumstances are.

—Abraham Lincoln

We have conducted thousands of hours of training, to include coverage of the material presented in this book, to private- and public-sector organizations worldwide. One of the key consumers of that training continues to be the CIA itself. Not long ago, on the second day of a three-day training course at the Agency, we opened the session as we always do by asking if anyone had any questions about Day One. A CIA officer we'll call "Ted" raised his hand and asked, "Does this stuff really work?" The question wasn't posed in a way that suggested Ted was particularly skeptical, but he did seem to be genuinely bothered.

"We never cease to be amazed at how well it works," Phil replied. "Why, is there something from yesterday that wasn't clear?"

"No, it's not that," Ted said. He went on to explain that the previous evening when his family had finished dinner, the kids went upstairs to do their homework, and he and his wife were still at the table having coffee. The phone rang, and they looked at each other, each hoping the other would get up and answer it. "Are you going to get that?" his wife asked. "Why don't you get it—it's probably your boyfriend," Ted said jokingly. At that point they realized that one of the kids had answered it, and it was obviously for one of them, as it typically was at that time in the evening. Ted laughed and said, "I guess it's not your boyfriend."

Then Ted dropped the bombshell on the class: When he said that to his wife, she exhibited a cluster of the very deceptive behaviors that the class had learned about the previous day. The issue confronting Ted was that he liked what he had heard on Day One, and it all made perfect sense to him. But now it was hitting him smack in the face, and it involved a situation that really mattered to him. He said he had been unable to sleep the entire night; he kept tossing and turning, wondering what to do. He would roll over and look at his wife, and think that there was just no way she could be cheating on him. Then he would roll back and think about friends whose spouses were found to have been unfaithful. What should he do? Should he just ignore it?

Phil threw the question out to the class. Should they tell Ted that he was probably being hypersensitive because he had just gone through the training, and advise him to let it go? Should they suggest that he start getting the names of good divorce attorneys? At that point, there was only one good piece of advice Phil could offer.

"Look at it this way," Phil said. "You have more work to do."

There was probably no more important takeaway for anyone who underwent the training. Identifying deceptive behavior doesn't make you a human lie detector, and it doesn't suddenly thrust you into the dual role of judge and jury. No question, you now have a very useful and effective tool that can help you resolve everyday situations involving deception. But it must be employed with the understanding that what it yields is information that warrants further examination.

An equally important takeaway is that while this information makes all of us better at *detecting* deception, it doesn't make any of us any better at *executing* deception. We've been doing this for a long time, and we can assure you that we're just as susceptible to the model as anyone else is. Certainly, there are things that occur to us that we can do to avoid waving a red flag. Susan will tell you that she has stricken "I swear to God" from her vocabulary, because invoking religion is such an obvious deceptive indicator. But she'll also tell you that she's just as likely to catch herself using convincing statements as she is to catch anyone else. Maybe she'll get overly specific. There are things we all do when we're uncomfortable with conveying truthful information, regardless of how well we know this stuff.

The reason we're all susceptible to the model is that there is so much conflicting information to process, and so many distinct behavioral elements to consider, that our brains simply can't keep track of them all. A good illustration of why it's so difficult is an old party-game challenge that you and your friends may have tried as kids.

While seated, extend your right leg, and with your heel on the floor, rotate your foot in a clockwise direction. Now, with your right hand, draw the number 6 in the air. What just happened to your foot? Much more often than not, your foot will begin to rotate in the opposite direction without you even realizing the change. Sometimes your brain just does what it does, and you end up following along. The same thing will happen when you attempt to manipulate your own deceptive behavior. Your brain will get in the way just about every time.

Perhaps this will also allay any concerns you might have had about bad guys reading this book and learning how to lie more successfully. Our methodology for detecting deception is structured around the way we're wired as human beings to respond to a stimulus. We can minimize or eliminate certain behaviors in our response, but other behaviors are still likely to manifest themselves, and they'll give us away.

We're often asked whether being in this field has had any impact on our family lives. Phil will tell you that for a long time, he was convinced that there was absolutely no connection—that what he did at work and what he did at home with his family were two nonintersecting worlds. That presumption would eventually get a reality check.

When their son Philip was a sophomore in high school, Phil and his wife, Debi, heard that Philip had his first steady girlfriend. Like many teenagers at that stage, Philip wasn't at all forthcoming with his parents about this development. Naturally, Phil and Debi were curious about this milestone in Philip's life, but they only had two bits of intelligence to work with: the name "Ashley," and the word "cheerleader."

Phil would occasionally drive Philip and some of his friends home from football practice in the family van, and on one such occasion Philip's best friend Ramon was sitting up front, and was talking to the guys in the back. Phil couldn't help but overhear Ramon mention the name "Ashley."

After a couple of minutes there was a lull in the conversation, and Phil looked over at Ramon. Very casually, being careful not to appear too eager, he asked his innocent question: "Ashley . . . is she a cheerleader?" Before Ramon could answer, Philip yelled out from the back of the van.

"Ramon, don't answer that!" he shouted. "It may *sound* like a harmless question!"

Busted.

Susan has learned that the kids pick up on a lot of this

stuff, too. Her daughter, Lauren, is now a teenager, and one day Lauren's boyfriend, Bobby, happened to mention to the family that his little sister Caroline had cut the whiskers on their dog. The family talked about how dumb that was because animals use their whiskers for sensory purposes, like being able to tell if they can fit through a small space.

About a week later, Lauren was playing with Sadie, the Carnicero family dog. She noticed that Sadie's whiskers had been cut, and some hair on her brow was missing, so she told her mom. Susan immediately suspected her preteen son, Nick, who was in Caroline's class and probably wanted to boast of the shared experience.

In the car on the way to church that Sunday, Lauren was driving, and Susan decided to confront Nick with the allegation. "Nick, why did you cut Sadie's whiskers and her eyebrow?" she asked. Nick's reaction was priceless.

"Mom, I swear to God, I did not touch her whiskers!" Nick declared. "You said dogs need their whiskers, so I wouldn't do that! You can put me on a polygraph! I swear on the Bible, I did *not* cut Sadie's whiskers!"

Without missing a beat, Lauren chimed in. "Invoking religion . . . overly specific . . . convincing statements . . ." Susan had to summon her professional bearing to prevent herself from laughing. She hadn't realized just how much her work had rubbed off on her daughter.

We've accepted that all of this is a part of our lives, and that while we don't live our lives in L-squared mode, reading behavior isn't something that's simply switched on and off. We've also learned that sometimes, that can be kind of a curse.

We have a good friend and colleague—we'll call him "Richard"—who has worked with the methodology for years, and who can read behavior as well as anyone we know. Richard recently had a medical condition that his physician suspected was cancer, and recommended that a minor surgery be performed in order to do a biopsy on the suspect tissue. Richard had gotten a second opinion from a doctor who doubted it was cancer, so we all had good reason to be hopeful that the biopsy would show that it was just a minor medical ailment.

Richard had an appointment with his physician eleven days after the surgery to get the results. When that interminable wait was over and Richard went to the doctor's office, he soon had reason to be concerned. He could sense from some of the behaviors the nurse exhibited upon his arrival that the news wasn't going to

DO:

- Practice—a lot. Watch talk shows, interview shows, news programs, any forum in which people are called upon to respond to questions. To use a golf analogy, we've taught you how to grip and swing the club. How good your game gets depends entirely on how much you practice.

- Refrain from practicing on your significant other.

- Use your new skills only for good.

DON'T:

- Do or say anything that makes the person aware that you're reading him, because it will trigger his defenses. For example, don't confront the person with your observation that he exhibited a particular deceptive behavior. If you tell him you spotted an anchor-point movement, he'll do his best to keep still for the remainder of the encounter, and you've lost what might have been a very valuable tool.

- Allow yourself to deviate from the cluster rule or from a focus on the behaviors we've outlined. Getting overly aggressive doesn't work—you'll see an eyelash flutter and you'll be ready to say, "Book 'em, Danno."

- Ask the question unless you're sure you really want to know the answer.

be good. He was even more certain of that within a few seconds of being greeted by the doctor.

Richard knew that just as the first thing out of the mouth of a truthful person who's been accused of wrongdoing is normally an explicit and forceful denial, if the doctor had good news to share, that likely would have been the first thing he would say to Richard. Instead, the doctor invited Richard to have a seat, and asked how the surgery to remove the tissue was healing.

If there's a curse to being able to read someone's behavior, it's that it can lead us to a place where we'd rather not go. We all have needs, desires, and hopes about how life will turn out for us, and that reality affects us when we read people—it's why in so many cases we desperately want to believe them. The situations that arise in our everyday lives usually don't lend themselves to a clinical, dispassionate analysis. There's a human element involved that often makes learning the truth extremely difficult to wrestle with.

But what we need to keep in mind is that in the end, knowing the truth is almost always in our best interest.

Richard, indeed, was diagnosed with cancer. It was an unpleasant truth, but it was the truth. And it was a reminder that truth, unpleasant or not, matters. Burying his head in the sand would not have been Richard's best course of action. With the truth available to him, he was able to plan the course of action that he needed to take in order to win the battle that confronted him.

As he walked across the atrium of the CIA's headquarters building to pick up his afternoon polygraph subject on that summer day in the early 1980s, Phil glanced at the huge Agency seal embedded in the marble floor. Like it had done on any number of previous occasions, the seal evoked two thoughts: first, how fortunate and proud he felt to be an employee of the Central Intelligence Agency; second, how incredulous he was that he had fallen into a career in which he would be depended upon to know when someone is lying.

On that day, Phil faced the most challenging examinee that he'd so far encountered in his young career. The subject was a psychologist—we'll call him "Dr. Smith"—who had applied for a position with the Agency's Office of Medical Services. Although well credentialed, Dr. Smith had a disturbing arrogance about him. And there was something else beyond the cavalier attitude that was unsettling. Phil couldn't put his finger on it, but he had learned to listen to what his gut was telling him. This was going to be a grueling session.

In the course of the polygraph pre-test, Dr. Smith admitted to no wrongdoing other than limited past use of marijuana, but Phil could sense that the man was concealing something because he was especially uncomfortable with questions relating to criminal activity. Phil found himself focusing on the behaviors Dr. Smith exhibited in response to those questions, an almost surreal situation that pitted a young, relatively inexperienced polygraph examiner against an accomplished, Ivy League–educated psychologist in a behavioral analysis showdown.

It would be years before Phil would extensively chart those behaviors and conceive of a methodology to analyze them, but early on he knew he had an advantage when it came to identifying deception. His track record had proven it. Still, could he hope to win when matched up against this seasoned psychologist? Surely, this doctor was capable of playing mind games. What dark secret did he have, and could he keep it successfully concealed?

Phil was convinced that the psychologist was lying when he claimed that he had not engaged in criminal activity as an adult, and he began to focus his questions in that area. As the questioning progressed, Dr. Smith's behavior was betraying him. And then came the admission: Dr. Smith had on a number of occasions told paraplegic patients that their paralysis was in their minds, and that with his help, they could walk. He would then prop them against a wall and tell them to push away, all for the delight of seeing them fall helplessly to the floor. The respected, seemingly accomplished psychologist who was seeking employment with the Central Intelligence Agency was in dire need of therapy himself.

No doubt, the particular questions Phil asked, and the manner in which he asked them, were the utensils that extracted Dr. Smith's confession. What's important to appreciate here is that even before we had fully developed the deception-detection methodology or the question formulation and interview strategies that we've shared with you in this book, relatively primitive versions of those tools were used with stunning success under circumstances with far-reaching and potentially grave consequences. The information you now have at your disposal represents a manifold increase in effectiveness and applicability compared to what Phil had to work with when he confronted Dr. Smith.

There's something else that's important to leave you with. People sometimes ask us how we've managed to spend our careers encountering not only the likes of Dr. Smith, but others who have committed some of the most horrific acts imaginable, without becoming hopelessly jaded and sullen, and downbeat about where we as a society are heading.

Part of it has to do with a steadfast refusal to sit in judgment of anyone. Rare are the individuals who can say truthfully they wouldn't dearly love to have a do-over in some aspect of their lives, and we don't pretend to be among them. Even fewer are the people who have ever walked the Earth without telling a lie. So we're happy to leave the judgment of other people to the judicial process. Our mission is solely to uncover the truth by employing the deception-detection model, and the interviewing and noncoercive interrogation techniques associated with it.

But perhaps the more essential reason is that for all the bad in humanity that we've seen in this job, we've seen far, far more good. Having had the immense good fortune of serving with countless people who have devoted their lives to the safety and security of our country and of our fellow human beings around the world, we have seen way too much selfless dedication and genuine sacrifice to ever be anything but uplifted by our experiences in this line of work. If this book helps you to capture that spy-the-lie moment and to thereby identify untruthfulness in people, let it also serve to reinforce the fact that good people in all walks of life do good things every day to fix the problems that deception creates. Let's never allow ourselves to forget how undeniably true that statement is.

APPENDIX I

Suggested Question Lists

Since the model we've presented in this book relies so heavily on the particular questions you ask to stimulate the behavior you want to analyze, we've compiled question lists for several scenarios to assist with your question formulation. We've found these questions to be enormously effective in their respective scenarios, and to be useful in serving as a guide for question formulation in other situations. Don't think of any of these as a checklist—the order and choice of questions will vary depending on the circumstances of the particular encounter and your own preferences. Also note that in each scenario, it's helpful to use a catch-all question.

I.I. QUESTIONS TO ASK WHEN HIRING A CAREGIVER FOR CHILDREN

There may be no interview experience that's more critically important to get right than one that involves a search for someone to care for your children. In addition to an in-depth interview (in a two-parent household, both parents should take part), a background investigation should be conducted that, at minimum, includes a criminal history check (including a check of national and local sex offender registries) and a thorough check of references, including at least one developed reference (a reference that is not provided by the interviewee).

At some point during the interview, you should introduce the prospective caregiver to your child, even if the child is an infant. Does your child seem uncomfortable around the prospective caregiver? Children seem to be born with an innate sense of whom they feel protected with, so take that into consideration. Always listen to your instincts as you evaluate the manner in which the caregiver engages your child or holds your infant. Are you comfortable with the level of gentleness and care displayed by the caregiver? If your child is an infant, does the interviewee make appropriate adjustments to the baby's clothing and surroundings? Her willingness to make those adjustments is important, because it reflects a "baby first" mentality. Does she ask questions that appropriately reflect interest in the baby's welfare and familiarity with the baby's needs? As you make those observations, consider asking the interviewee these questions:

- Why did you become a caregiver for children?
- How long have you worked as a caregiver?
- What ages have you cared for?
- What age children have you enjoyed caring for the most? Why?
- What ages have you felt or would you feel uncomfortable caring for? Why?
- Have you cared for both genders?
- Is there any reason that your name would appear on any sex offender registry?
- What do you find most rewarding about being a caregiver?
- What do you like least about being a caregiver?
- Tell me about the most difficult child (infant) you have ever cared for.
- What is the biggest challenge you have faced in caring for a child (infant)?
- How long should an infant cry before you check on it?
  - » Follow-up: Why? (Ask the caregiver to explain why she would handle the situation in the manner she described.)
- How long should you let an infant cry before you pick it up?

» Follow-up: Why? (Ask the caregiver to explain why she would handle the situation in the manner she described.)

- What is your philosophy for disciplining children?
- What is the harshest discipline you have ever handed out as a caregiver?
- What is the most significant emergency situation you have handled as a caregiver?
- What first-aid or emergency training have you had?
- What was the most difficult family you have ever had to work with?
  » Follow-up: Why were they difficult?
  » Follow-up: In hindsight, what might you have done differently to make that situation a better experience for all involved?
- What aspects of being a caregiver do you find frustrating?
- What do children (infants) do that might cause you to lose your temper?
- When is the last time you recall losing your temper, or coming close, when caring for a child?
- What type of child do you find is the most difficult to care for?
- What is the worst experience you've had when you were responsible for a child?
- What will your references say is your biggest strength as a caregiver?

- What will your references say is your biggest weakness as a caregiver?
- Under what circumstances would you give in to a child's wishes or demands about something that the parents have expressly forbidden?
- Is there any reason that any of your references will have any hesitation in recommending you as a caregiver?
- What haven't I asked you that you think I should know about?

I.II. QUESTIONS TO ASK YOUR CHILD ABOUT USING DRUGS AND ALCOHOL

When questioning your child or teen about potential drug and alcohol use, it's very important to do so in a low-key, non-accusatory manner. That will help you to maintain a positive relationship with the child, and increase your level of confidence that any behaviors you observe are stimulated by the question, and not by what your child perceives as an aggressive or threatening demeanor. As your child begins to talk to you, refrain from reacting, or being judgmental. If you think you may not be able to do that, consider asking another family member or close friend to have the conversation, possibly someone closer to the child's age. Also, it's important that you not question your child at a time when you suspect he's under the influence of drugs or alcohol, because you can't be certain of the reliability of the behavioral indicators you observe.

It is also important to refrain from immediately drilling down on any admissions your child makes. For example, if your child admits experimentation with marijuana, you should resist the urge to ask a series of follow-up questions about that experimentation. Instead, accept the admission, then set it aside for a few moments and simply ask what other drugs the child has tried. But do it without alerting the child to how deep you plan to drill on each admission. That way, you will keep his defenses down and be much more likely to gain a more complete picture of the totality of the drug use. After you have captured that picture, you're ready to begin drilling down. Start with his last admission first. That was likely the most serious, and the one he was most reluctant to share with you. By getting the most difficult issue out of the way first, your questioning becomes easier for the child to accept. Here are some questions to serve as a guide (you can substitute "alcohol" for "drugs" where appropriate). You should phrase the questions in a way that's natural and consistent with how you normally communicate with your child.

- What types of drugs seem popular? (This is an important question to ask early on, because it will give you some sense of your child's familiarity with the drug culture in his world.)
- What kinds of drugs have you been offered?

- What kinds of drugs have you actually seen?
- What kinds of drugs have you experimented with?
- What kinds of drugs have you been most tempted to try?
- What kinds of drugs have you seen your friends taking?
- What is the drug situation like at school (in the neighborhood)?
- Is there any reason any of your friends would tell their parents that you have used drugs?
- Were you ever surprised to see drugs at a party or on another occasion?
- Were you ever surprised to learn that one of your friends was using drugs?
- How would you feel about being asked to take a drug test?
- On a scale of one to ten, one being "not at all" and ten being "almost did it," what is the most you have been tempted to try a drug of any type?
- Under what circumstances could you see yourself trying some type of drug?
- What haven't I asked you that you think I should know about?

I.III. QUESTIONS ABOUT MATTERS OF INFIDELITY

Infidelity is a topic that should never be approached lightly, or be the subject of idle conversation. Always remember that broaching the issue with your spouse or significant other, guilty or not, can be a very emotionally charged situation. If you're going to be successful, you need to manage your own emotions to the very best of your ability, and remain as calm as you can possibly be. When asking these questions, you want to ensure that the behavior you observe is in response to the question, and not a visceral reaction to your demeanor. Although this is an extraordinarily difficult issue to deal with, do your best not to appear to ambush the other person. Instead, you might lead into the conversation by first expressing some self-doubt that you might be having, possibly a wistful reference to your appearance or aging. Don't initiate the conversation by attacking the person with statements like, "You don't love me anymore," or "You're no longer interested in me." Those statements will likely trigger your spouse's defenses, which may color the behavioral responses to your questions. Do your best to prevent the interaction from deteriorating into an argument. That will close the door on your quest for information.

If your spouse admits to an episode of infidelity, accept the admission without reacting, and simply ask what other times this has happened. Keep asking "what other times" until your spouse either provides a denial devoid of any deceptive behavior, or it appears clear that you're dealing with psychological entrenchment. Now you're ready to drill down on the specific occurrences, beginning with the last admission first. That's likely to be the one that's the most serious.

Keep in mind that you're not going to ask all of the questions listed here. Just pick the ones that best apply to your situation. One more piece of advice: Be absolutely certain that you want to know the answer to the question before you ask it.

- Who have you found yourself especially attracted to? Why?
- When is the last time you were tempted to have an affair?
- What really happened between you and (name of individual in question)?
- Is there any reason that someone would say you're having an affair?
- Since our relationship began (Since we got married . . .), who else have you been sexually active with?
- When is the last time you had sex with someone besides me?
- Do you have an emotional attachment to anyone else?
- Under what circumstances would you ever consider having an affair?
- When is the last time someone came on to you (hit on you)?
  » Follow-up: What did that lead to?
- What haven't I asked you that you think I should know about?

I.IV. QUESTIONS TO ASK IN THEFT SITUATIONS

The range of possibilities in theft situations is almost limitless. People take all sorts of things, from money to material goods to secrets. It's impossible to develop a list of specific questions that would be appropriate in all theft cases, but there are some key concepts that can be addressed in most theft situations, which enable the questioner to get a better sense of the person's culpability. Obviously, this list is not intended to cover the entire scope of questions in a theft investigation. But the concepts underlying the following questions can be helpful, and the questions can be modified to address most theft situations.

- What do you know about the missing _____ (money, computer, car, etc.)?
- What involvement did you have in the disappearance of the missing _____?
- Where is the missing _____ now?
- Is there any reason that security cameras would show you in the vicinity of the missing _____ before it was taken?
- Is there any reason someone would say he saw you at the location where the missing _____ was taken?
- Is there any reason we will find your fingerprints in the area where the missing _____ was taken?

- When is the last time you were in the area where the missing _____ was taken?
- Is there any reason a forensic investigation would yield evidence that points to you as the person who took the missing _____?
- As a sign of good faith, would you be willing to reimburse the loss out of your own pocket? (If the person isn't culpable, his likely response will be something like, "You're out of your mind! I didn't take the money, so why on earth would I do that?" The culpable person may not agree to do it, but he might agree to think about it. If the response is something like "I don't know, that's interesting . . . I'd have to think about that," consider that a red flag.)
- What haven't I asked you that you think I should know about?

APPENDIX II

A Sample Narrative Analysis Based on the Model

When this book went to publication, Jerry Sandusky, a former assistant football coach at Pennsylvania State University, had been arrested twice within one month on charges of sexual abuse of young boys. He was arrested on November 5, 2011, and charged with forty counts of abusing eight boys, and was freed on $100,000 bail. Sandusky was arrested again on December 7, after two more alleged victims came forward with accusations that he had molested them. He was freed on $250,000 bail the next day, and was confined to his home and ordered to wear an electronic monitor.

On November 14, NBC's Bob Costas interviewed Sandusky by phone, and on November 17, we posted our analysis of that interview. We are providing that analysis here as an example of how we employ the model to prepare a narrative analysis for the public.

It is important to point out that, as of the time of writing, Sandusky had denied the charges, had pled not guilty, and had been found guilty of none of them. This analysis represents nothing more than our opinions based on our observation of Sandusky's behavior in this interview, and should not be construed in any way as proof that Sandusky is guilty of any of the charges. With that understood, here's the analysis we prepared:

SUMMARY: *The nature of the allegations that former Penn State assistant football coach Jerry Sandusky molested or had sexual involvement with multiple minors has led many to believe that Sandusky is likely guilty of most, if not all, of those allegations. Our behavioral assessment of Sandusky's November 14 interview with NBC's Bob Costas strongly supports that conclusion. What is even more disturbing, however, is that our analysis also suggests that Sandusky's improper contact with children may not be limited to those cases alleged in the indictment. He displays a very high volume of deceptive indicators in the interview, and his consistent failure to provide denials to direct questions regarding the matter is particularly noteworthy.*

What follows is the complete transcript of the interview, which Costas conducted with Sandusky by phone. It includes a segment with Sandusky's attorney, Joseph Amendola, who was in the studio with Costas for his portion of the interview. Our behavioral analysis is appended to Sandusky's responses.

Costas: Mr. Sandusky, there's a forty-count indictment, the grand jury report contains specific detail, there are multiple accusers, multiple eyewitnesses to various aspects of the abuse. A reasonable person says, "Where there's this much smoke, there must be plenty of fire." What do you say?

Sandusky: I say that I am innocent of those charges.

ANALYSIS: *In his opening question, Costas in essence is telling Sandusky that he considers the allegations in the indictment to be true, which means to Sandusky that Costas believes he must have molested the children in question. Instead of directly denying those allegations, Sandusky says, "I'm innocent of those charges." In behavioral analysis, such a statement is termed a false denial. A more direct denial would have been, "I never molested any of those kids." Sandusky's statement relates to a legal outcome rather than serving as a denial that he molested the children. As we all know, there have been numerous cases in which guilty people have been found innocent, even when there is overwhelming evidence to the contrary.*

Our assessment is that, like many people who appear deceptive, Sandusky may be having a hard time telling the more direct lie, "I didn't do it." If he knows he molested the children, it's easier for him to make the more indirect statement that he's "innocent," perhaps even with the hope that a less-than-savvy jury might reach that verdict.

Costas: Innocent? Completely innocent and falsely accused in every aspect?

Sandusky: Well, I could say that, you know, I have done some of those things. I have horsed around with kids, I have showered after workouts. I have hugged them and I have touched their leg without intent of sexual contact. But, um, so if you look at it that way, there are things that would be accurate.

ANALYSIS: *Apparently finding that Sandusky's previous response lacks credibility, Costas challenges him to determine whether he's saying or implying that nothing in the indictment is true. Sandusky's response contains a number of deceptive behaviors, and also appears to contain a significant unintended message regarding his culpability in the matter. When Sandusky begins his response with, "Well, I could say that, you know, I have done some of those things," our assessment of the statement is that he knows that most, if not all, of the allegations in the indictment are true, making it psychologically difficult to deny everything. Thinking that he will have to make some admissions, probably knowing there is significant evidence to support the allegations in the indictment, he probably believes he is simply admitting to behavior that may be questionable, but is not illegal. Based on the model, this opening* statement in his response strongly suggests otherwise. We see the potential unintended message here that he did molest the children. That, coupled with his admissions that he showered with them and touched them, is the equivalent of placing Sandusky at the scene of the crime. From a behavioral standpoint, the interview already is not going well for Sandusky.

Costas: Are you denying that you had any inappropriate sexual contact with any of these underage boys?

Sandusky: Yes, I am.

ANALYSIS: *Costas appears to have the best of intentions by continuing to drill down rather than let Sandusky off the hook. Unfortunately, Costas incorporates the language of a direct denial into his question, which lets Sandusky off the hook to a degree, because he only has to agree with the denial rather than having to actually say it. From a behavior-assessment standpoint it would have been much more interesting if Costas had asked, "What sexual contact or involvement did you have with these kids?" If Sandusky had once again failed to respond with a direct denial, it would have been very damning in terms of his culpability.*

Costas: Never touched their genitals? Never engaged in oral sex?

Sandusky: Right.

ANALYSIS: *Again, kudos to Costas for his persistence in his efforts to confirm inappropriate sexual contact between Sandusky and the children. However, he again lets Sandusky off the hook to a degree by asking a negative question, which leaves Sandusky with no option but to agree. In fairness, Costas may have switched from the information-collection mode to an approach that would lock Sandusky into a story that sounds ludicrous to the public.*

> **Costas:** What about Mike McQueary, the grad assistant who in 2002 walked into the shower where he says, in specific detail, that you were forcibly raping a boy who appeared to be ten or eleven years old? That his hands were up against the shower wall and he heard rhythmic "slap, slap, slap, slapping" sounds—and he described that as a rape?

> **Sandusky:** I would say that that's false.

ANALYSIS: *Based on the model, we conclude that Sandusky's response is extremely deceptive. His failure once again to express a direct denial, perhaps something to the effect of "I didn't rape the boy," or even "I didn't have any sexual contact with him," coupled with his statement, "I would say that that's false," leaves us with little doubt that the incident occurred just as McQueary described it. Sandusky doesn't claim that McQueary's allegation is actually false, or that the incident didn't happen. Instead, he goes only so* *far as to state what he "would say" in response to the allegation. Collectively, these two deceptive indicators clearly suggest that the incident alleged by McQueary most likely took place.*

Costas: What would be his motive to lie?

Sandusky: You'd have to ask him that.

ANALYSIS: *Sandusky's response here contains two significant deceptive indicators. First is his reluctance to address the question; second is his failure to deny any sexual involvement with the boy. This behavior strongly reinforces our analysis of Sandusky's response to the previous question.*

Costas: What did happen in the shower the night that Mike McQueary happened upon you and the young boy?

Sandusky: Okay, we were showering and horsing around and he actually turned all the showers on and was actually sliding across the floor and, as I recall, possibly like snapping a towel in horseplay.

ANALYSIS: *Our analysis leads us to conclude that by stating or implying he doesn't remember, Sandusky is trying to make it difficult for the interviewer to continue his pursuit of the truth.*

Costas: In 1998 a mother confronts you about taking a shower with her son and inappropriately touching him. Two detectives eavesdropped on her conversations with you and you admit that "maybe your private parts touched her son." What happened there?

Sandusky: Well, I can't exactly recall what was said there. In terms of what I did say was that if he felt that way, then I was wrong.

ANALYSIS: *In this exchange, our behavioral analysis suggests, Sandusky is acknowledging in a roundabout way that he did have sexual contact with the youth in question, and that the contact was of a nature that was "wrong." Also, his selective memory ("Well, I can't exactly recall what was said there") is to us a clear demonstration of a behavioral ploy to avoid having to provide incriminating specifics.*

Costas: During one of those conversations you said, "I understand. I was wrong. I wish I could get forgiveness," speaking now with the mother, "I know I won't get it from you. I wish I were dead." A guy falsely accused or a guy whose actions have been misinterpreted doesn't respond that way, does he?

Sandusky: I don't know. I didn't say, to my recollection, that I wish I were dead. I was hopeful that we could reconcile things.

ANALYSIS: *With this question, Costas is saying to Sandusky that his responses, and the behavior associated with those responses, indicate that he is guilty of the allegations against him. Instead of offering a blanket denial, Sandusky only takes issue with one small point made by Costas by claiming that he didn't recollect saying, "I wish I were dead." His continued failure to directly and forcefully deny the allegations is very disturbing from a behavioral point of view, and continues to indicate, based on our application of the model, the strong probability that Sandusky is guilty.*

> **Costas:** Shortly after that in 2000, a janitor said that he saw you performing oral sex on a young boy in the showers in the Penn State locker facility. Did that happen?
>
> **Sandusky:** No.

ANALYSIS: *Interestingly, now that Costas has pointed out to Sandusky that his behavior and responses lack credibility, Sandusky appears to recognize the need to be more direct in response to a specific allegation. He therefore simply says, "No." Without realizing it, Costas may have significantly and artificially altered Sandusky's behavior by alerting him to the unacceptability of his responses.*

> **Costas:** How could somebody think they saw something as extreme and shocking as that when it hadn't

occurred, and what would possibly be their motivation to fabricate it?

Sandusky: You'd have to ask them.

ANALYSIS: *Costas continues his persistence, and refuses to accept Sandusky's "No" for an answer. When challenged on the issue raised in the previous question, Sandusky reverts back to his habit of failing to make any sort of denial, and instead tries to evade Costas by pointing him toward the janitor. Collectively, Sandusky's responses, based on our application of the model, strongly indicate, again, that he is guilty.*

Costas: It seems that if all of these accusations are false, you are the unluckiest and most persecuted man that any of us has ever heard about.

Sandusky: I don't know what you want me to say. I don't think that these have been the best days of my life.

ANALYSIS: *Apparently frustrated by Sandusky's less-than-credible responses in the face of what appears to be very credible evidence, Costas is sarcastic in articulating his suspicions. Even in the face of such blatant sarcasm, Sandusky again fails to specifically deny molesting any of the children. He also makes what is probably a very truthful statement when he says, "I don't think that these have been the best days of my life." If Sandusky is*

guilty of the allegations levied against him, as our behavior as-
sessment suggests, then he has good reason to feel that these are
not his "best days."

Costas (narrating): Sandusky's attorney, Joseph Amendola, insists the charges filed by the Commonwealth of
Pennsylvania listing eight victims will not hold up.

Costas: You said a few days ago, "Much more is going
to come out in our defense." In broad terms, what?

Amendola: We expect we're going to have a number of
kids—now, how many of those so-called eight kids we're
not sure—but we anticipate we're going to have at least
several of those kids come forward and say this never
happened, this is me, this is the allegation, and it never
occurred. In fact, one of the toughest allegations—the
McQueary allegations—what McQueary said he saw,
we have information that that child says that never
happened. Now grown up.

Costas: Until now we were told that that alleged victim could not be identified. You have identified him?

Amendola: We think we have.

Costas: So you found him, the Commonwealth has not?

Amendola: Yeah. Interesting, isn't it?

Costas: Would you allow your own children to be alone with your client?

Amendola: Absolutely. I believe in Jerry's innocence. Quite honestly, Bob, that's why I'm involved in the case.

Costas: You believe in his innocence? Not just that you can mitigate his guilt, you believe in his innocence.

Amendola: I believe in his innocence.

Costas (narrating): Meanwhile, the man who helped Joe Paterno win national championships is now at the center of a scandal that's brought his old boss down.

Costas: To your knowledge, did Joe Paterno have any information regarding objectionable activities on your part prior to that report in 2002?

Sandusky: I can't totally answer that question. My answer would be, "No."

ANALYSIS: *Sandusky's qualified statement that he "can't totally answer that question" indicates to us that there is indeed informa-*

tion regarding "objectionable activities" that Sandusky believes Paterno was aware of prior to 2002.

Costas: Did Joe Paterno at any time ever speak to you directly about your behavior?

Sandusky: No.

Costas: Never?

Sandusky: No.

Costas: He never asked you about what you might have done?

Sandusky: No.

Costas: He never asked you if you needed help, if you needed counseling?

Sandusky: No.

Costas: Never expressed disapproval of any kind?

Sandusky: No.

ANALYSIS: *Sandusky did not exhibit any deceptive indicators in the exchange related to whether or not Paterno spoke to him directly about any of his alleged objectionable behavior. However, the absence of deceptive indicators could be the result of Costas's use of negative questions, which gave Sandusky an easy out (see chapter 11).*

Costas: How do you feel about what has happened to Penn State, and to Joe Paterno, and to the Penn State football program, and your part in it?

Sandusky: How would you think that I would feel about a university that I attended, about people that I've worked with, about people that I care so much about? How do you think that I would feel about it? I feel horrible.

Costas: You feel horrible. Do you feel culpable?

Sandusky: I'm not sure I know what you mean.

ANALYSIS: *Costas has been very persistent in his pursuit of the truth, and once again questions Sandusky regarding his culpability. Sandusky again fails to deny any culpability, and even expresses a lack of understanding of the question. Based on the model, his behavior continues to point to his likely culpability.*

Costas: Do you feel guilty? Do you feel as if it's your fault?

Sandusky: No, I don't think it's my fault. I obviously played a part in this.

ANALYSIS: *In response to the question of whether this matter is his fault, Sandusky makes inconsistent statements. First, he makes the qualified statement, "I don't think it's my fault." Then he appears to reverse himself by saying, "I obviously played a part in this." Based on our analysis, the inconsistency indicates to us Sandusky's awareness that these allegations are true, and he is finding it very difficult to position himself as someone who hasn't done anything wrong.*

Costas: How would you define the part you played? What are you willing to concede that you've done that was wrong and that you wish you had not done?

Sandusky: Well, in retrospect, I shouldn't have showered with those kids.

Costas: That's it?

Sandusky: Yeah. Well, I mean, that's what hits me the most.

ANALYSIS: *When asked what wrongdoing he is willing to concede to, Sandusky admits that he "shouldn't have showered with those kids." Again, that places him at the equivalent of the crime scene. This, coupled with the extremely high volume of deceptive indicators throughout the interview suggests to us that there is much more to the story than has surfaced to date.*

Costas: Are you a pedophile?

Sandusky: No.

ANALYSIS: *Although there are no deceptive behaviors exhibited here, it is important to note that Costas has posed an opinion question to Sandusky, who may have rationalized his behavior to be something less than what meets the threshold of being a pedophile.*

Costas: Are you sexually attracted to young boys, to underage boys?

Sandusky: Am I sexually attracted to underage boys? Sexually attracted? No. You know, I enjoy young people. I love to be around them. But no, I'm not sexually attracted to young boys.

ANALYSIS: *Sandusky exhibited significant deceptive behavior in response to this question. He repeats the question twice in what* *appears to be an attempt to buy himself some time so that he can formulate what he thinks might be an acceptable response.*

> **Costas:** Obviously you are entitled to a presumption of innocence, and you'll receive a vigorous defense. On the other hand, there is a tremendous amount of information out there, and fair-minded, common-sense people have concluded that you are guilty of monstrous acts. And they are particularly unforgiving with the type of crimes that have been alleged here. And so, millions of Americans who didn't know Jerry Sandusky's name until a week ago now regard you not only as a criminal, but—I say this I think in a considered way—but as some sort of monster. How do you respond to them?

> **Sandusky:** I don't know what I can say or what I could say that would make anybody feel any different now. I would just say that if somehow people could hang on until my attorney has a chance to fight, you know, for my innocence, that's about all I could ask right now. You know, obviously it's a huge challenge.

ANALYSIS: *Even in the face of being labeled a "monster," Sandusky can't seem to muster the gumption to deny the extraordinarily serious allegations made against him. In addition, his statement, "I don't know what I can say or what I could say that would make anybody feel different now," indicates to us Sandusky's inevitable* realization that it's very difficult to get people to believe a lie. That's especially the case when it involves something as heinous as the allegations he will have to face in the months, and perhaps years, ahead.

GLOSSARY

Anchor point—Any part of the body that anchors a person to a particular spot or position, including the feet, which are always anchor points. We look at anchor point movement as a potential nonverbal deceptive behavior in which anxiety is dissipated through the physical movement.

Attack behavior—A deceptive verbal behavior in which a person attacks the questioner, the victim, or any third party as a means of compelling the questioner to back off from a particular line of questioning. This often takes the form of attempting to impeach the credibility or competence of the questioner. Example: "How long have you been doing this job?"

Autonomic nervous system—The part of the nervous system that controls the functions of body organs and involuntary physical reactions to stimuli.

Bait question—A question that establishes a hypothetical situation and is designed to trigger a "mind virus" in the mind of a deceptive person. Bait questions typically begin with the phrase, "Is there any reason that . . ."

Baselining—Comparing observed behavior with an established norm. This is a behavior-assessment strategy that we recommend be avoided because of the high potential for drawing a faulty conclusion.

Behavioral pause/delay—A nonverbal deceptive behavior in which a silent gap of time precedes a person's response to a question.

Catch-all question—A wrap-up question that is designed to uncover lies of omission, and to serve as a safety net in the event that the questioner inadvertently overlooks an issue. Example: "What haven't we discussed that's important for me to know about?"

Closed-ended question—A question that's used to gather specific case facts. Example: "Who was already in the office when you arrived this morning?"

Cluster—Any combination of two or more deceptive indicators.

Compound question—A question type that is to be avoided because it contains more than one question, making behavioral analysis of the response difficult due to potential confusion over what part of the question is causing the deceptive behavior. Example: "How frequently do you go running, and where do you typically run?"

Convincing statement—A true or irrefutable statement made in an effort to convince the accuser and to influence his perception, rather than to convey information that addresses the facts of the case. Example (when asked if the person took the missing money): "I'm an honest person, I would never do that."

Denial—A statement in response to a question, usually regarding an act of wrongdoing, that asserts that an allegation is false.

Denial problems—A category of deceptive verbal behavior in which a person appears to have a problem with denying an allegation. This can take the form of failing to deny the allegation altogether, providing a nonspecific denial (example: "I would never do something like that"), or providing an isolated delivery of the denial by burying it in a long-winded answer.

Exclusion qualifier—A deceptive verbal behavior used to enable a person who wants to withhold certain information to answer a question, but without disclosing all of the information. Examples: "basically," "for the most part," "fundamentally," "probably," "most often."

Failure to answer—A deceptive verbal behavior in which a person's response does not answer the question that's asked.

Failure to understand a simple question—A deceptive verbal behavior in which a person's response is an expression of confusion over an easily comprehensible question. This strategy is typically used when a person feels trapped by the wording of the question and needs to shrink its scope.

Fight-or-flight response—A triggering of the autonomic nervous system that reroutes circulation to the body's major organs and muscle groups to prepare the body to deal with a threatening situation.

Global behavior assessment—A behavior assessment strategy that focuses on capturing and analyzing all types of behavior, rather than focusing on specific deceptive behaviors exhibited in response to a question.

Grooming gesture—A nonverbal deceptive behavior in which anxiety is dissipated through physical activity in the form of grooming oneself or the immediate surroundings.

Hand-to-face activity—A deceptive nonverbal behavior in which a person touches his face or head region in response to a question, which can be prompted by discomfort associated with circulatory changes triggered by the fight-or-flight response.

Hiding mouth or eyes—A deceptive nonverbal behavior in which a person uses a hand to shield his mouth or eyes when responding to a question, or closes his eyes when responding to a question that does not require reflection.

Inappropriate level of concern—A deceptive verbal or nonverbal behavior in which a person attempts to equalize the exchange by diminishing the importance of the matter at hand. He may focus on either the issue or the process. Verbal example: "Why is everybody making such a big deal about this?" Nonverbal example: Smiling or chuckling in response to a question regarding a grave situation.

Inappropriate level of politeness—A deceptive verbal behavior in which a person interjects an overly polite or unexpectedly kind or complimentary comment directed at the questioner when responding to a question. Example: uncharacteristic use of "sir" or "ma'am" when responding to a particular question.

Inappropriate question—A deceptive verbal behavior in which a person responds with a question that doesn't directly relate to the question that's asked. Example: In response to the question, "Is there any reason we would find your fingerprints on the missing laptop?" a person asks, "How much did it cost?"

Inconsistent statement—A deceptive verbal behavior in which a person makes a statement that is inconsistent with what he said previously, without explaining why the story has changed.

Invoking religion—A deceptive verbal behavior in which a person makes a reference to God or religion as a means of "dressing up the lie" before presenting it. Example: "I swear on a stack of Bibles, I wouldn't do anything like that."

Leading question—A question that contains the answer that the questioner is looking for.

Legitimacy statement—A statement in a question prologue designed to explain why the question needs to be asked.

Lie of commission—A lie that is conveyed definitively by means of making a statement that is untrue. Example: A person who has stolen the missing money says, "I didn't take the money."

Lie of influence—A lie that is conveyed by means of attempting to manipulate perception rather than to provide truthful information.

Lie of omission—A lie that is conveyed by means of withholding statements that would disclose the truth.

L-squared mode—Using one's visual and auditory senses to *look* and *listen* simultaneously in order to observe both verbal and nonverbal deceptive behaviors as they're exhibited in response to a question.

Microexpression—An involuntary, split-second movement of facial muscles that conveys an emotion such as anger, contempt, or disgust. We recommend avoiding reliance on microexpressions, due to their impracticality and the fact that there is no microexpression for deception.

Mind virus—A colloquial term for the psychological discomfort a person feels when he receives information that has potentially negative consequences, causing his mind to race with hypothetical ramifications of the information.

Minimization—An element of a question prologue designed to minimize the perception of negative consequences that may be associated with a truthful response to the question.

Negative question—A question that is phrased in a way that negates an action. This question type is to be avoided because it conveys an expectation of a response that potentially lets the person off the hook. Example: "You didn't flirt with her, did you?"

Nonanswer statement—A deceptive verbal behavior in which a person responds to a question with a statement that does not answer the question, but rather buys him time to formulate a response that he hopes will satisfy the questioner. Example: "That's a very good question."

Nonverbal deceptive indicator—Any deceptive behavior that is exhibited in response to a question and that does not involve verbal communication.

Open-ended question—A question that is asked as a means of establishing the basis for a discussion or to probe an issue, and which generally solicits a narrative response. Example: "What were you doing in Las Vegas when you were supposed to be visiting your mother in Tampa?"

Opinion question—A question that solicits a person's opinion as a means of assessing his likely culpability in a given situation. The "Punishment Question" falls into this category. Example: "What do you think should happen to a person who dines in a restaurant and leaves without paying?"

Overly specific answer—A deceptive verbal behavior in which the person's response is too narrow and technical at one extreme, or too detailed and exhaustive at the other.

Perception qualifier—A deceptive verbal behavior employed to enhance credibility. Examples: "frankly," "to be perfectly honest," "candidly."

Presumptive question—A question that presumes something related to the matter under discussion or investigation.

Process/procedural complaint—A deceptive verbal behavior in which a person takes issue with the proceedings. It may be a delaying tactic or an attempt to steer the proceedings down a different path. Example: "How long is this going to take?"

Projection of blame—An element of a question prologue designed to encourage a person to be less defensive by suggesting that the blame for the matter at hand does not rest exclusively with him.

Psychological alibi—An attempt to deceive through the use of selective memory or ostensibly limited knowledge.

Psychological entrenchment—The condition in which a person feels compelled to dig his heels in the ground and stick to his story, making the information collection process especially difficult.

Question prologue—A short, narrative explanation preceding a question that is designed to prime the information pump, so that if the person is on the fence about whether or not he's going to give you something, it will help to influence him to come down on your side of the fence.

Rationalization—An element of a question prologue designed to encourage a person to open up by suggesting that there is a socially acceptable reason that to some degree might excuse the activity under investigation.

Referral statement—A deceptive verbal behavior in which a person refers to a previous statement or message. This takes advantage of repetition as a psychological tool that can make the questioner more open to a possibility than he otherwise might have been.

Reluctance/refusal to answer—A deceptive verbal behavior in which a person displays discomfort, reticence, or unwillingness to answer the question.

Repeating the question—A deceptive verbal behavior in which a person repeats the question he's asked as a means of buying time to formulate his response.

Selective memory—A deceptive verbal behavior in which a person creates a psychological alibi by responding to a question with a stated inability to remember.

Stimulus—Any question or statement that prompts a behavioral response.

Throat-clearing/swallowing—A nonverbal deceptive behavior in which a person clears his throat or performs a significant swallow prior to answering the question.

Timing—The guideline in our deception-detection model dictating that the initial deceptive behavior must begin within the first five seconds after the stimulus.

Unintended message—A truthful statement made by a deceptive person that, when the literal meaning of the statement is analyzed, conveys information that the person does not realize he's conveying. We also refer to this as "truth in the lie."

Vague question—A question to be avoided because it allows for excessive latitude in the response.

Verbal deceptive indicator—Any deceptive behavior that involves verbal communication in response to a question.

Verbal/nonverbal disconnect—A deceptive behavior in which a person's verbal and nonverbal behaviors in response to a question don't match. A common verbal/nonverbal disconnect in Western cultures occurs when a person nods affirmatively while saying "No," or turns his head from side to side while saying "Yes."

ABOUT THE AUTHORS AND WRITER

THE AUTHORS

Philip Houston, Michael Floyd, and Susan Carnicero are founding partners in QVerity (www.qverity.com), a company that provides training and consulting services worldwide in deception detection, screening, and interviewing techniques.

Phil Houston

Phil is a nationally recognized authority on deception detection, critical interviewing, and elicitation. His twenty-five-year career with the Central Intelligence Agency was recognized with the award of the Career Intelligence Medal, and was highlighted by his service as a senior member of the Office of Security. In that capacity he conducted thousands of interviews and interrogations for the CIA and other federal agencies, both as an investigator and as a polygraph examiner. He is credited with developing a detection of deception methodology currently employed throughout the U.S. intelligence and federal law enforcement communities. The scope of Phil's work has covered criminal activity, personnel security, and key national security matters, including counterintelligence and counterterrorism. The fact that many of his interviews were conducted in foreign countries, coupled with six years of residence overseas, has given him unique insight and extensive experience in dealing with foreign cultures.

The story of Phil's success in creating a commercial application and market for the detection of deception methodology was featured in the 2010 book, *Broker, Trader, Lawyer, Spy* by Eamon Javers. He holds a B.A. in political science from East Carolina University in Greenville, North Carolina, where he and his wife, Debi, still live.

Michael Floyd

Michael provides training and consulting services for Forbes Top 10 families and large corporations throughout North America, Europe, and Asia. He is widely recognized as a leading authority on interviewing, detection of deception, and elicitation in cases involving criminal activity, personnel screening, and national security issues.

Michael is the founder of Advanced Polygraph Services, where he spent ten years conducting high-profile interviews and interrogations for law enforcement agencies, law firms, and private industry. He has most recently been involved in providing training and consulting services in the areas of detection of deception and information collection to firms in the financial services and audit communities.

Michael began his career as a commissioned officer in the U.S. Army Military Police, serving in the United States and Asia. He subsequently served with both the Central Intelligence Agency and the National Security Agency. Throughout a career that has spanned more than thirty-five years, he has conducted more than eight thousand interviews and interrogations worldwide.

A graduate of the University of South Dakota with a B.S. in education, Michael also holds an M.S. degree in detection of deception from Reid College, and a JD degree from Seattle University School of Law. Michael and his wife, Estelita Marquez-Floyd, M.D., live in Napa, California.

Susan Carnicero

A former security specialist with the Central Intelligence Agency, Susan has twenty years of experience in interviewing, interrogation, and polygraph examination, focused primarily on national security, employment, and criminal issues. Susan is the developer of a behavioral screening program currently used within the federal government and in a variety of private industries. She is widely considered a leading authority on interviewing, detection of deception, and elicitation.

Susan has extensive experience in conducting training for federal government agencies and the law enforcement community, as well as for financial services firms and other private-sector companies. Most recently, she has been involved in conducting high-level screening interviews within the U.S. government, and in providing consulting services for Forbes Top 10 families.

Prior to joining the CIA, Susan served in the investor relations and corporate communications field, where she achieved the position of director of public relations for a Fortune 500 company.

Susan holds a B.A. in communications from George Mason University in Fairfax, Virginia, and an M.A. in forensic psychology and M.A. in secondary education/English from Marymount University in Arlington, Virginia. She lives in Chantilly, Virginia, with her daughter, Lauren, and son, Nicholas.

ABOUT THE AUTHORS AND WRITER

The Writer

A veteran business/technology journalist and now a partner in QVerity, **Don Tennant** began his career with the National Security Agency as a research analyst covering international economic issues. His experience in producing key intelligence reports for senior U.S. policymakers prepared him for a venture into journalism, which led to his appointment as editor in chief of *Computerworld,* and later to the editorial directorship of *Computerworld* and *InfoWorld.* Don has conducted indepth interviews with hundreds of top corporate executives and dozens of high-profile CEOs.

Don was presented with the 2007 Timothy White Award for Editorial Integrity by American Business Media, and he is a recipient of the prestigious Jesse H. Neal National Business Journalism Award for editorial excellence in news coverage. He has received several national gold awards for his editorial columns in *Computerworld.*

Don holds a B.S. in language (cum laude) from Georgetown University in Washington, D.C. He and his wife, Ardith, live on the campus of Green Acre Bahá'í School in Eliot, Maine. Follow him on Twitter: @dontennant.

INDEX

INDEX